PRAYERSCRIPTS
Speaking God's Word Back To You

STANDING IN THE GAP for THE PRESIDENT

★ ★ ★ ★ ★

50 Days of Prayer for

★ **LEADERSHIP** ★ **LOYALTY** ★ **LIFELINE** ★

CYRIL OPOKU

Standing in the Gap for The President: 50 Days of Prayer for Leadership, Loyalty, and Lifeline

© 2025 Cyril Opoku. *PrayerScripts*. All rights reserved.

No part of this publication may be reproduced, stored in a retrieval system, or transmitted in any form or by any means—electronic, mechanical, photocopy, recording, or otherwise—without the prior written permission of the publisher, except in the case of brief quotations used in reviews, articles, or devotionals.

Published by *Quest Publications*

ISBN: 978-1-988439-63-1
Cover design by *Quest Publications (questpublications@outlook.com)*

Unless otherwise indicated, all Scripture quotations are taken from the World English Bible (WEB), which is in the public domain. For more information, visit: www.worldenglish.bible

This book is a work of devotional encouragement. It is not intended to replace biblical study, pastoral counsel, or professional therapy.

Printed in the United States of America.

First Edition: July 2025

For more books like this, visit *PrayerScripts:* https://prayerscripts.org

Contents

Preface .... *vi*
Introduction .... *vii*
How to Use This Book .... *x*

SECTION 1: PRESIDENTIAL CHARACTER & LEADERSHIP 1
Day 1:   Anoint the Chief 2
Day 2:   Heart of Wisdom 3
Day 3:   Humble Leadership 4
Day 4:   Strength for His Day 5
Day 5:   Guard His Steps 7
Day 6:   Heart of Compassion 9
Day 7:   Discernment in Counsel 10
Day 8:   Courage in Crisis 11
Day 9:   Vision from Above 13
Day 10: Shield His Mind 15
Day 11: Voice of Truth 17
Day 12: Spirit of Integrity 19
Day 13: Faithful in Small Things 21
Day 14: Boldness to Speak 23
Day 15: Prayer for His Family 25
Day 16: Protection in the Heights 27
Day 17: Guided by God's Counsel 29

SECTION 2: AGAINST DISLOYAL INSIDERS 31
Day 18: Expose the Traitor 32
Day 19: Bind Their Tongues 34
Day 20: Shield the Trustworthy 36

Day 21: Purge the Wicked Council 38
Day 22: Destroyed By Their Perverseness 40
Day 23: Guard Against Deception 42
Day 24: Wisdom to Detect Lies 43
Day 25: Root Out Hidden Schemes 45
Day 26: Deliver from Betrayal 47
Day 27: Don't Let Them Rejoice 49
Day 28: Silence the Whisperers 51
Day 29: Protect the Faithful 52
Day 30: Guard the Nation's Secrets 54
Day 31: Exile the Faithless 56
Day 32: Expose Hidden Motives 58
Day 33: Uphold Those of Good Conscience 60
Day 34: God, Our Refuge from Treachery 62

SECTION 3: AGAINST ASSASSINATION ATTEMPTS 64
Day 35: Help Against the Killers 65
Day 36: Shadow of Death, Fear Not 67
Day 37: Vaulted in God's Arms 69
Day 38: Watchtower over Our Head 71
Day 39: No Hurt Shall Come 73
Day 40: Frustrate Wicked Devices 75
Day 41: Eyes Guarding Day and Night 77
Day 42: God Is Our Refuge 79
Day 43: Encompassed by His Wings 81
Day 44: Divine Escort on the Way 83
Day 45: Prolong the King's Life 85
Day 46: Hidden from the Snare 87
Day 47: Guarded by Angels 89

Day 48: Exposed Schemes Foiled 91
Day 49: No Unlawful Plot Prevails 93
Day 50: Safe in His Care 95

Epilogue *97*
Encourage Others with Your Story *99*
More from PrayerScripts *100*

Preface

In times of national uncertainty, spiritual darkness, and global unrest, the burden to intercede for leadership becomes not just a calling—but a divine mandate. *Standing in the Gap for The President: 50 Days of Prayer for Leadership, Loyalty, and Lifeline* was birthed from a sacred urgency to pray strategically, fervently, and scripturally for the highest seat of influence in our land: the President.

This is not a political book, nor is it bound by party lines or personal preferences. It is a spiritual war manual. It is a clarion call to those who understand the weight of intercession, the necessity of godly leadership, and the consequences of spiritual passivity. The soul of a nation often hinges on the heart of its leaders. Therefore, we must labor in prayer that righteousness, wisdom, protection, and divine guidance prevail in the life of the President and those surrounding him.

Each prayer in this book was crafted with intentionality—anchored in Scripture, rich in prophetic insight, and saturated with the passion of an intercessor's cry. The days ahead are filled with both challenge and promise, but we are not powerless. We have been given spiritual authority through Christ to stand in the gap.

May this book ignite your prayer life, deepen your resolve, and awaken a generation of watchmen on the walls who will not hold their peace day or night. May you be strengthened to intercede with boldness, accuracy, and endurance—believing that God hears, God sees, and God responds to the cries of His people.

For His glory,
Cyril O.
Illinois, July 2025

INTRODUCTION

Leadership is not merely a position—it is a spiritual battleground. Every decision made at the highest levels of government echoes across families, communities, and generations. When the President leads with wisdom, integrity, and courage, the nation is blessed. But when compromise, confusion, or corruption invade the seat of power, the consequences are swift and far-reaching. That is why intercession is not optional; it is essential.

Standing in the Gap for The President: 50 Days of Prayer for Leadership, Loyalty, and Lifeline is a sacred journey for those called to pray with purpose and precision. It is for intercessors, leaders, pastors, patriots, and anyone who believes in the power of prayer to shape the destiny of a nation. This is not casual devotion—it is a call to spiritual warfare.

Throughout Scripture, God searched for those who would "stand in the gap" before Him on behalf of the land (Ezekiel 22:30). He looked for men and women who would intercede—not for personal gain, but for divine alignment. Today, He is still searching. He is looking for those who will carry the burden of national leadership in prayer, not just in times of crisis, but consistently and intentionally.

This book is divided into three focused sections:

- **Section 1: Presidential Character & Leadership** – Prayers that address the inner life, wisdom, strength, and moral integrity of the President.
- **Section 2: Against Disloyal Insiders** – Strategic intercession to expose betrayal, preserve trust, and uphold righteous counsel within the administration.

- **Section 3: Against Assassination Attempts** – Warfare prayers for divine protection against physical, spiritual, and political attacks meant to destroy the President's life or assignment.

Each day contains a Scripture-based prayer that is designed to engage the heart of God, declare His Word, and release divine intervention. These prayers are not driven by fear, but by faith. Not by political agendas, but by heaven's assignment.

As you walk through these 50 days, may the Holy Spirit lead you deeper into a place of authority and compassion. May you pray not just *for* a man, but *through* the heart of God for the preservation of a divine plan. You are not just reading prayers—you are joining an army of intercessors who believe that God still governs in the affairs of men, and that nations can still be turned by those who dare to pray.

Let us stand in the gap together. The future depends on it.

A Word About Authority and Honor

Intercessors sometimes wrestle with frustration toward leaders or systems. This guide intentionally cultivates a posture of honor—not excusing injustice, but praying from a place of respect for God-ordained authority (Romans 13:1). Change that flows from honor carries heaven's fragrance; criticism birthed in bitterness rarely bears righteous fruit.

Invitation to Partnership

This book is not an end in itself; it is a tool for partnership. Pair it with fasting. Gather a few friends on a video call. Print the daily Scriptures and post them in your workplace. Use it as a 50-day sprint, a weekly prayer rhythm, or a small-group study. The design is modular so churches, prayer groups, and individuals can adapt it to their context. Ask your pastor if your church can spend a month in focused intercession for the nation's leader. God loves to answer united, scriptural prayer.

Final Charge

As you embark on this 50-day journey, don't underestimate the power of your prayers. You are not just reading words on a page—you are standing in the gap, partnering with heaven, and declaring God's purposes over a nation in need. This is holy work. Stay faithful, stay focused, and stay expectant. Let your voice rise like incense before the throne, knowing that the God who hears is also the God who heals. May you be strengthened for the days ahead, bold in your intercession, and unwavering in your faith. Now, take your place on the wall—your nation needs your prayers.

How to Use This Book

This book is designed to be a 50-day prayer journey of intercession for the President, based on God's Word and guided by the Holy Spirit. Whether you are praying individually, with a small group, or leading a church-wide initiative, here's how to make the most of each day's entry:

1. Set Aside a Daily Time for Prayer

Consistency matters. Choose a quiet time each day to focus, pray, and reflect. Mornings are ideal for many, but any time of day that allows you to pray without distraction will work.

2. Read the Daily Theme and Scripture

Each day includes a clear theme that targets a specific area of need in the nation. Read the accompanying Scripture slowly and prayerfully. Let the Word speak to your spirit before you begin to pray.

3. Pray the Written Prayer Aloud or Silently

The prayers provided are deeply rooted in Scripture and crafted to express the heart of an intercessor. Pray them aloud or in silence—either way, let the words become your own as you lift them before God with faith and sincerity.

4. **Add Your Own Intercession**

   Use the written prayers as a launching pad for your own intercession. Name your city, your leaders, your concerns. Let the Spirit lead you to pray beyond the page. Feel free to journal what the Lord shows you during your time in prayer.

5. **Gather Others to Pray with You**

   Though you can use this book alone, it becomes even more powerful when used in unity with others. Consider inviting friends, family, or your church to take the 40-day journey together. You may even want to host weekly gatherings or online prayer check-ins.

6. **Believe and Expect Results**

   This isn't a religious exercise—it's a faith-filled mission. As you pray, expect God to move. Watch for changes, both spiritual and tangible. Remember, God is listening, and He is faithful to His Word.

Let this be a holy assignment. You are standing in the gap for a nation under God—and your prayers are making a difference.

SECTION 1:
PRESIDENTIAL CHARACTER & LEADERSHIP

In this opening section of *Standing in the Gap for The President: 50 Days of Prayer for Leadership, Loyalty, and Lifeline*, we focus our hearts and prayers on the very foundation of effective and godly leadership—the character and integrity of the President. True leadership begins not with policy or position, but with the inner man or woman who governs with wisdom, humility, and a heart devoted to God.

As we stand in the gap, we recognize that the strength of a nation flows directly from the moral compass and spiritual grounding of its highest leaders. The prayers in this section invite the Holy Spirit to shape the President's character, fortify his integrity, and guide his decisions according to God's perfect counsel. We seek not only capable governance but a leadership marked by godliness, courage, and unwavering commitment to truth.

May these prayers open the door for divine transformation, so that our President leads with a heart aligned to heaven, a mind disciplined by Scripture, and a spirit empowered by grace. Together, we intercede for a leader who reflects God's righteousness and whose example inspires a nation toward justice, peace, and lasting unity.

Day 1: ANOINT THE CHIEF

> Then Samuel took the vial of oil, and poured it on his head, and kissed him, and said, "Hasn't Yahweh anointed you to be prince over his inheritance?
> —1 Samuel 10:1 WEB

Sovereign Lord, God of Israel and King above all kings, we come humbly before You, crying out on behalf of our nation's leader. As Samuel took the flask of oil and poured it on Saul's head, declaring, "Has not the Lord anointed you ruler over His inheritance?"—so we ask, O God, that You would stretch out Your hand and anoint the one who stands in the seat of presidential authority.

You are the One who raises up and brings down. You search hearts and test motives. You know the burdens that rest on the shoulders of leadership, and You alone can provide the strength, humility, and wisdom required to govern Your people well. So, we ask—anoint the Chief.

Set apart the President for righteousness. Let every decision be guided by Your Spirit. Surround him with counselors who fear You, and remove every voice that seeks to corrupt or derail Your purposes. Cause him to lead with courage and integrity, to value justice and mercy, and to recognize that the office he holds is not his own—it belongs to You, the Ruler of nations.

Let this anointing not be for show, but for service. Transform his heart, align his will with Yours, and let the oil of Your Spirit flow over every word, every policy, every moment of governance. Raise him up not just as a leader of a nation, but as a servant of the Most High God.

In Jesus' name, Amen.

Day 2: HEART OF WISDOM

> But if any of you lacks wisdom, let him ask of God, who gives to all liberally and without reproach; and it will be given to him.
> —James 1:5 WEB

Gracious and all-wise God,

You are the fountain of wisdom, the One who gives generously without finding fault. Today, we stand in the gap for the President of this nation, asking for what You have so freely promised—wisdom from above. Your Word says that if anyone lacks wisdom, they should ask, and it will be given. So we ask boldly, humbly, and urgently on behalf of our nation's leader: pour out wisdom like a river that never runs dry.

Grant the President a heart that hungers for Your truth above the praise of people. Silence every voice that does not align with Your will, and raise up wise counselors who speak with clarity, courage, and conviction. Strip away pride, confusion, and fear, and replace them with discernment rooted in reverence for You. In every decision—foreign or domestic, moral or legislative—let Your wisdom prevail.

Where there is pressure, be the calm. Where there is temptation, be the guardrail. Where there is uncertainty, be the anchor. Lord, we cry out for leadership not driven by politics, polls, or power—but by Your Spirit. May righteousness, justice, and mercy shape every policy and proclamation.

We entrust the President to You—not because of human strength, but because You are sovereign, and Your purposes will stand. Lead him in paths of wisdom for the sake of the people, the nation, and Your glory.

In Jesus' name, Amen.

Day 3: Humble Leadership

> He has shown you, O man, what is good. What does Yahweh require of you, but to act justly, to love mercy, and to walk humbly with your God?
> —Micah 6:8 WEB

Lord God Almighty, Ruler of the nations, You have shown us what is good. You have made clear what You require: to act justly, to love mercy, and to walk humbly with You. So now we come, standing in the gap for our President, pleading for a heart that bows before You—not in pretense, not in pride, but in true humility.

Lord, tear down every tower of arrogance, every high wall of self-sufficiency, and replace them with the fear of the Lord—which is the beginning of wisdom. Raise up in our leader a heart that listens more than speaks, that seeks counsel before giving commands, and that trembles at Your Word more than public opinion.

May justice not be a performance, but a conviction. Let mercy not be a slogan, but a lifestyle. And let humility not be a weakness, but the strength that draws its power from You. Shield our President from the seduction of applause and the addiction to control. Instead, may he walk closely with You—daily, dependently, and delighting in Your ways.

You are the true King, and we ask that our President governs as one under authority. Break what must be broken, build what must be built, and lead him to lead us rightly. For the sake of Your name, and the healing of our land.

In Jesus' name, Amen.

Day 4: STRENGTH FOR HIS DAY

> He gives power to the weak. He increases the strength of him who has no might. Even the youths faint and get weary, and the young men utterly fall; But those who wait for Yahweh will renew their strength. They will mount up with wings like eagles. They will run, and not be weary. They will walk, and not faint.
> —Isaiah 40:29-31 WEB

Mighty and Everlasting God,

You are the One who gives power to the faint and strength to those with no might. Today, we stand in the gap for the President, lifting him before Your throne of grace. You see the weight he carries—the unseen burdens, the pressures of leadership, and the battles he must face behind closed doors. Lord, when he grows weary, renew his strength. When his vision dims, lift his eyes to You, the Maker of heaven and earth.

Your Word says that even young men shall stumble and fall, but those who wait on You shall renew their strength. Father, teach him to wait on You—not on the polls, not on approval, not on the plans of man. Teach him to abide in You, to draw from the well of Your wisdom and the depth of Your peace. Help him rise on wings like eagles above division, discouragement, and deception. Empower him to run his race with endurance and not grow weary, to walk the long path of leadership and not faint.

Clothe him in integrity, surround him with truth, and uphold him with Your righteous right hand. Strengthen him not just for the tasks of the day, but for the calling of his soul—to serve as a leader under Your authority. Let him not lean on his own understanding, but in all his ways acknowledge You, and You will direct his path.

In Jesus' name, Amen.

Day 5: GUARD HIS STEPS

> A man's goings are established by Yahweh. He delights in his way. Though he stumble, he shall not fall, for Yahweh holds him up with his hand.
> —Psalms 37:23-24 WEB

Lord God, Righteous Judge and Faithful Shepherd,

We lift up the President of this nation before You, the One who orders the steps of those who delight in You. Your Word says that the steps of a good man are established by the Lord, and though he may stumble, he will not be cast down—for You uphold him with Your hand. So, Father, we ask that You guard his steps.

Order them in Your truth. Lead him away from deceitful counsel and into the path of righteousness. Plant his feet on steady ground—free from compromise, fear, or pride. In the weight of leadership, when decisions grow heavy and the pressures of power press in, steady his soul with Your peace.

Let him not be swayed by applause or intimidation, but let him walk in holy conviction, governed by Your Spirit. When he falters, lift him with Your mercy. When he grows weary, strengthen him with Your might. And when darkness surrounds, shine Your light and make his path clear.

Raise up voices of wisdom around him, those who revere You and walk uprightly. Shield him from the snares of the wicked, from every pit dug in secret. And may his leadership reflect the fear of the Lord, the beginning of all wisdom.

We intercede for him not as perfect, but as one in need of Your hand—one whom You can use to lead a people back to You. Guide him. Guard him. And use him for Your glory.

In Jesus' name, Amen.

Day 6: Heart of Compassion

> Put on therefore, as God's chosen ones, holy and beloved, a heart of compassion, kindness, lowliness, humility, and perseverance; bearing with one another, and forgiving each other, if any man has a complaint against any; even as Christ forgave you, so you also do.
> —Colossians 3:12-13 WEB

Righteous Father, You who sit enthroned in justice and mercy, we come before You today, standing in the gap for the one who leads this nation. According to Your Word in Colossians 3:12–13, You have called us as Your chosen ones to clothe ourselves with compassion, kindness, humility, gentleness, and patience. So we ask, Lord, that You would place these very garments upon the heart of our President.

Shape his character, O God, in the image of Christ. Let him not lead from pride or self-interest, but from a well of mercy that mirrors Yours. Let his decisions be bathed in compassion for the weak, the vulnerable, and the voiceless. In a world that often rewards hardness of heart, give him the courage to be tender where others are callous, patient where others are impatient, and humble where others exalt themselves.

Teach him, Lord, to forgive as You have forgiven us. Where offenses rise and conflicts mount, remind him that true leadership walks the higher road of grace. Guard his soul against bitterness and pride. Let him be quick to listen, slow to speak, and slow to become angry.

Cover him with Your Spirit. Let compassion not be a fleeting feeling but a holy conviction that governs his thoughts, his tone, his policies, and his leadership. May his example draw this nation not toward division, but toward healing.

In Jesus' name, Amen.

Day 7: DISCERNMENT IN COUNSEL

> Where there is no wise guidance, the nation falls, but in the multitude of counselors there is victory.
> —Proverbs 11:14 WEB

Righteous Father,

You are the source of all wisdom, the Counselor who never errs, and the Sovereign who governs in perfect justice. Today, we humbly come before You on behalf of the one who leads our nation. Your Word declares, "Where there is no guidance, a people falls, but in an abundance of counselors there is safety" (Proverbs 11:14). We cling to this promise and ask that You would surround our President with voices rooted in truth, integrity, and reverence for You.

Silence every lying tongue and hidden agenda. Expose every motive that seeks selfish gain rather than national good. Raise up wise advisors—men and women who fear You, love righteousness, and understand the times. May their counsel be like fresh water, cleansing confusion and bringing clarity. Let Your Spirit stir the President's heart to discern not only the good, but the best—Your will above all.

In moments of pressure, let there be stillness to hear Your whisper. In times of crisis, give the courage to act with bold humility. And in every decision, big or small, may godly counsel prevail over popularity, and Your truth stand taller than any political ambition.

Have mercy on our land, Lord. Guide our leader by Your hand. Keep his heart tethered to truth, that our nation may be kept from falling.

In Jesus' name, Amen.

Day 8: COURAGE IN CRISIS

> Haven't I commanded you? Be strong and courageous. Don't be afraid. Don't be dismayed, for Yahweh your God is with you wherever you go."
> —Joshua 1:9 WEB

Mighty God, Sovereign over the nations,

We come before You with humbled hearts, standing in the gap for the one You have appointed to lead this nation. You have said in Your Word, *"Have I not commanded you? Be strong and courageous. Do not be afraid; do not be discouraged, for the Lord your God will be with you wherever you go."* And so, Lord, we boldly lift up the President, asking that You would clothe him with divine courage in every crisis and challenge he faces.

Let not fear or confusion take root in his heart. Let not the weight of public opinion, political pressure, or the threats of man shake his resolve. Instead, let Your presence be his anchor. May he rise each day with the assurance that You are with him, not as a distant observer, but as a near and present guide—leading him through every valley and storm.

Father, strengthen him with the spirit of Joshua—undaunted by opposition, unwavering in conviction, and yielded fully to Your commands. When decisions loom large and burdens grow heavy, breathe fresh courage into his soul. Guard his heart from discouragement, and let him not be swayed by the winds of fear, but led by the still, strong voice of Your Spirit.

Surround him with godly counsel, Lord—voices that speak truth, not flattery; wisdom, not confusion. And when the path ahead seems uncertain, remind him that You are already there. You go before him, and You are with him. Let that be his confidence.

Raise him up, Lord, as a leader who walks in courage not for show, but in obedience to Your Word. Let his leadership be marked by righteousness, by bold faith, and by decisions that reflect Your justice and mercy.

We declare, in alignment with Your Word, that he will not be afraid. He will not be dismayed. For the Lord his God is with him wherever he goes.

In Jesus' name, Amen.

Day 9: VISION FROM ABOVE

> Where there is no revelation, the people cast off restraint; but one who keeps the law is blessed.
> —Proverbs 29:18 WEB

Righteous Father, Maker of heaven and earth,

We come before You with hearts bowed low, lifting up the office of the President before Your holy throne. Your Word declares in Proverbs 29:18 that *"where there is no vision, the people perish: but he that keepeth the law, happy is he."* Lord, we cry out for heavenly vision—a vision that does not come from the wisdom of men, but from the counsel of Your Spirit.

Grant the President divine insight, not born of politics or pressure, but breathed from above. Let the eyes of his understanding be opened to see what You see—to discern the direction You desire for this nation under God. When the way is clouded with confusion or the noise of many voices, speak louder through Your Word and whisper wisdom into his soul.

Lord, raise up in him the heart of a true leader—one who fears You, walks uprightly, and seeks not popularity but purpose. Where ambition threatens clarity, refine his motives. Where pressure mounts, anchor him in Your peace. Let the laws he upholds be just, and the vision he casts bring unity, not division—hope, not despair.

We ask, O God, that You surround him with godly counsel—men and women who walk in the fear of the Lord and are not swayed by self-interest. Let their wisdom reinforce his own, and let Your Spirit direct every decision at every turn.

Where there is temptation to compromise, Lord, fortify his convictions. Where fatigue dulls discernment, awaken him with renewed strength. May he lead not from the seat of power, but from the posture of humility—always looking up for direction, always bowing low in reverence.

And for this nation, Father, we plead: let Your vision be restored across every branch of government, every house of leadership. Let Your people flourish under righteous rule. May truth rise again in our streets because our leaders see clearly through Your eyes.

We stand in the gap and ask You to plant heaven's vision in the heart of the President—for where there is no vision, the people perish.

In Jesus' name, Amen.

Day 10: SHIELD HIS MIND

> Let your gentleness be known to all men. The Lord is at hand. In nothing be anxious, but in everything, by prayer and petition with thanksgiving, let your requests be made known to God. And the peace of God, which surpasses all understanding, will guard your hearts and your thoughts in Christ Jesus.
> —Philippians 4:5-7 WEB

Righteous Father,

We come before You with reverence and urgency, standing in the gap for the one You have appointed to lead this nation. Let Your gentleness be evident through his life, as You have commanded in Your Word. In a time of pressure and division, we plead for Your peace to anchor his thoughts, and for Your presence to guard his heart.

Shield the mind of our President, Lord. Let him not be swayed by fear, confusion, or pride. Let Your Spirit whisper truth in the chambers of his soul. When anxiety knocks, let him turn to You in prayer and supplication, with thanksgiving, and may he experience the peace that surpasses all understanding. We ask You to post heavenly guards at the gates of his mind—against deception, against despair, against the spirit of manipulation.

Make him a man who is not reactionary, but responsive to You. Train him in righteousness, that his leadership may reflect integrity, humility, and wisdom from above. Let him be known not by political gain but by spiritual grounding. Let his decisions be born from a mind at peace—not from chaos or confusion, but from the counsel of the Holy Spirit.

Father, surround him with godly advisors, those who seek Your will above theirs. We pray that distractions and lies would be silenced, and Your truth would rise louder in his mind than every opposing voice. May his leadership flow from a sound mind, governed by Your Word and kept steady by Your peace.

You said the Lord is near. Be near to him now. Be near in every decision. Be near in every crisis. Be near in every moment of silence when he searches for clarity. Let Your nearness be his confidence and his lifeline.

We entrust his mind to Your keeping, O God who never sleeps nor slumbers. Shield it. Renew it. Fill it. And guard it with the unshakable peace of Christ.

In Jesus' name, Amen.

Day 11: Voice of Truth

You will know the truth, and the truth will make you free."
—John 8:32 WEB

Righteous Father, the One who reigns in truth and justice,

We come before You on behalf of our President, lifting up a cry that reaches beyond politics and power—into the heart of leadership that reflects Your character. You have declared in Your Word that *"You shall know the truth, and the truth shall make you free"* (John 8:32). Lord, we ask that Your truth would be the foundation upon which our President stands. Let every word spoken from his lips be sifted by Your Spirit, aligned with what is right in Your eyes—not shaped by pressure, fear, or the counsel of the ungodly.

We intercede, O God, for a voice that is not swayed by popular opinion, but one tuned to the frequency of Your voice—the voice of truth. Guard his heart from deception and the snares of flattery. Let integrity and uprightness preserve him, for he puts his trust in You. Raise up within him a deep reverence for Your Word and an unshakable commitment to speak truth, even when it costs.

Father, expose every lie whispered in secret places and silence every tongue that promotes falsehood around him. Surround him with counselors who love truth, who speak with wisdom, and who fear Your name more than they fear men. Let the President's character be a beacon of righteousness, leading by example and governed by conviction.

May his leadership reflect the truth of Christ—bold, compassionate, and unyielding to corruption. Set him apart in this generation as one who leads not for applause but for the advancement of what is just, what is noble, and what is true. Let him know the freedom that only Your truth brings, and may that freedom ripple through our nation.

We pray this with urgency, with hope, and with unwavering faith in Your sovereign hand.

In Jesus' name, Amen.

Day 12: SPIRIT OF INTEGRITY

> By David. Judge me, Yahweh, for I have walked in my integrity. I have trusted also in Yahweh without wavering. Examine me, Yahweh, and prove me. Try my heart and my mind. For your loving kindness is before my eyes. I have walked in your truth.
> —Psalms 26:1-3 WEB

Righteous Father, Judge of all the earth,

We lift up the one who stands as President over this nation, and we cry out for a deep and enduring work of integrity in his heart. Just as David declared, *"Vindicate me, O Lord, for I have walked in my integrity,"* we ask You to birth and sustain in our President a life led by truth, guided by Your unwavering standard, and tested in the fire of Your presence.

Search his heart, Lord. Examine his mind and soul, as David opened himself before You and said, *"For I have walked in Your truth and I have trusted in the Lord without wavering."* May the President not be swayed by the voices of flattery or the enticements of compromise. Strengthen him to stand firm when no one is watching, to choose right when wrong would be easier, and to fear You more than man.

Let Your lovingkindness be ever before him. Surround him with wise counsel that walks in Your ways, and deliver him from the traps of false alliances, hidden agendas, and deceitful lips. May he govern not with pretense, but with a clean heart and a clear conscience. Place within him a desire to please You above all, to walk humbly, to love mercy, and to act justly.

You see what is hidden in secret. You know the inner motives of every man. So we ask You, Lord, to purify the heart of our President and make him a vessel of honor, shaped by truth and led by grace. Uphold him by Your hand, for without You, no man can lead righteously.

Let the spirit of integrity not only rest upon him but ripple through every part of his leadership—his speech, decisions, alliances, and ambitions. Make his leadership a lifeline to righteousness and an example of loyalty to truth in a generation tossed by lies.

In Jesus' name, Amen.

Day 13: FAITHFUL IN SMALL THINGS

> He who is faithful in a very little is faithful also in much. He who is dishonest in a very little is also dishonest in much.
> —Luke 16:10 WEB

Righteous Father,

You are the God who examines the heart and weighs every motive. You see what is hidden and judge with perfect wisdom. Today, I stand in the gap for the one You have allowed to sit in the seat of presidential authority. Lord, You said in Luke 16:10 that *"whoever is faithful in very little is also faithful in much, and whoever is dishonest in very little is also dishonest in much."* I lift up the character and private decisions of the President before You—the unseen habits, the whispered thoughts, the quiet yes or no in small matters that reveal the truth of the heart.

Father, raise up in him a spirit of integrity that trembles before You. Teach him to honor You in the smallest judgments, the tiniest choices, the mundane tasks. Let his heart be tender to correction and quick to obey Your promptings, even when no one else is watching. May his leadership not be built on performance or popularity, but on faithfulness to You in the secret place.

Where there is compromise, confront it. Where there is pride, humble him. Where there is apathy, ignite fresh conviction. Let every decision he makes in the quiet set a foundation for righteous leadership in the public. Guard him from deception, from flattery, from shortcuts that erode character. Strengthen him to steward his authority with the fear of the Lord as his constant guide.

Lord, this nation needs a President whose private life mirrors the righteousness required for public trust. Make him faithful in the little so he may be found faithful in the much You've entrusted to him. Root his strength not in power, but in obedience. Not in image, but in truth. Not in ambition, but in service to Your will.

In Jesus' name, Amen.

Day 14: BOLDNESS TO SPEAK

> For God didn't give us a spirit of fear, but of power, love, and self-control.
> —2 Timothy 1:7 WEB

Righteous Father, Sovereign over all rulers and nations,

We come before You today standing in the gap for the one You have appointed to lead this nation. You have not given him a spirit of fear, but of power, love, and a sound mind. So, we ask, O God, clothe him in that truth. Let the spirit of holy boldness rise within him—a boldness not rooted in pride or human confidence, but in the deep assurance of Your calling and presence.

Where voices of intimidation threaten to silence what is right, give him courage to speak. Where compromise beckons, strengthen his spine to stand firm. May he not shrink back in the face of opposition, nor be swayed by polls or public pressure, but may he be anchored in the fear of the Lord, which is the beginning of wisdom.

Lord, baptize him afresh with Your Spirit. Let Your Word dwell richly in him, producing sound judgment and clarity in every decision. Surround him with counselors who fear You and embolden him to speak truth in love—even when it is unpopular, even when it costs.

Raise up in him the spirit of Daniel, who spoke boldly before kings. Give him the heart of David, who led with integrity and skillful hands. And give him the steadfastness of Paul, who declared, *"I am not ashamed of the gospel."* Let our President not be ashamed of righteousness, justice, or mercy, for these are the foundations of Your throne.

God of all wisdom and power, let his voice echo with heaven's authority. Make him a voice of truth in a confused generation, a leader unafraid to declare what is right, and a shepherd who speaks with compassion for the people he serves.

We plead this not for earthly glory, but that Your will be done in our land and Your name be honored once more in our nation.

In Jesus' name, Amen.

Day 15: PRAYER FOR HIS FAMILY

> Behold, children are a heritage of Yahweh. The fruit of the womb is his reward. As arrows in the hand of a mighty man, so are the children of youth. Happy is the man who has his quiver full of them. They won't be disappointed when they speak with their enemies in the gate.
> —Psalms 127:3-5 WEB

Lord God Almighty,

We come before You with humble hearts, lifting up the family of the President of this nation—those closest to him, those You have sovereignly placed around him as his inner circle, his home, his refuge, his most personal legacy. For Your Word declares in Psalm 127 that *"children are a heritage from the Lord, the fruit of the womb a reward."* You have said that *"like arrows in the hand of a warrior are the children of one's youth,"* and that *"blessed is the man whose quiver is full of them."* So we stand in the gap today, Lord, and ask You to bless and protect this man's household.

Shield his family, O God. Guard them from the constant assaults of public life—the scrutiny, the slander, the strain. May the President's home be a sanctuary of peace, not a battleground of pressure. May the bonds between husband and wife, between father and children, be strengthened by grace and not frayed by burdens. May love, respect, laughter, and wisdom dwell richly in his home.

Raise up in his household a standard of godliness. Let no weapon formed against his family prosper. Let no root of bitterness spring up, no distraction divide, no plan of the enemy take root. Pour Your Spirit upon his offspring and Your blessing on his descendants. Let the children and grandchildren of this leader rise and call him blessed—not just for his title, but for the integrity of his heart, the humility of his spirit, and the example of his love.

Let this man lead not only from podiums and platforms, but from the dinner table and the quiet moments of fatherhood. Let him be faithful in what is unseen as well as what is televised. For what profits a man to lead a nation, but lose his household?

We intercede, Lord—anchor his soul in You. Surround his marriage with covenant strength. Let every voice that seeks to divide be silenced, and let the voice of wisdom cry aloud in his home. Be the builder of his house, Lord, lest they labor in vain who build it.

In Jesus' name, Amen.

Day 16: Protection in the Heights

> He who dwells in the secret place of the Most High will rest in the shadow of the Almighty. I will say of Yahweh, "He is my refuge and my fortress; my God, in whom I trust." For he will deliver you from the snare of the fowler, and from the deadly pestilence. He will cover you with his feathers. Under his wings you will take refuge. His faithfulness is your shield and rampart. You shall not be afraid of the terror by night, nor of the arrow that flies by day; nor of the pestilence that walks in darkness, nor of the destruction that wastes at noonday.
> —Psalms 91:1-6 WEB

Most High God, who dwells in unapproachable light and covers Your own with the shadow of Your wings,

We come before You as watchmen on the wall, lifting up the President of this nation into Your secret place. You have said in Psalm 91 that "he who dwells in the shelter of the Most High will abide under the shadow of the Almighty." Father, let our leader be hidden in You—kept not by power or might, but by Your Spirit.

Shield him, O Lord, from the arrows that fly by day—the slander, manipulation, deception, and unjust attacks that seek to wear down his soul. Preserve him from the terror by night—every whispered threat, secret counsel, and spiritual assault intended to disturb his peace. You are our refuge and fortress, O God; be his fortress now. Let Your truth be his shield and buckler. Make him fearless—not in his own strength, but because he trusts in You.

We intercede for his thoughts, his decisions, his advisors, his sleep, and his schedule. May no pestilence of pride or compromise overtake him.

May no destruction that lays waste at noonday derail the plans You have for him to lead with righteousness, courage, and humility.

Surround him with songs of deliverance. Assign angels concerning him to guard him in all his ways. And even when he must stand in high places—under pressure and scrutiny—keep his footing firm and his spirit yielded to You. Let him not be swayed by the fear of man, nor seduced by the praise of man, but may he find protection, identity, and counsel in the secret place of the Most High.

Cover his household. Guard his heart. And through his leadership, let justice roll down like waters and righteousness like an ever-flowing stream in our land.

In Jesus' name, Amen.

Day 17: GUIDED BY GOD'S COUNSEL

> You will guide me with your counsel, and afterward receive me to glory.
> —Psalms 73:24 WEB

Righteous Father,

You who reign in wisdom and truth, we lift up the office of the President before You. You, O Lord, have declared in Your Word, *"You guide me with Your counsel, and afterward You will take me into glory"* (Psalm 73:24). We pray today that Your divine counsel would be the anchor and compass of the President's heart. Not the counsel of men, not the sway of polls, nor the pressure of politics—only the steady, unwavering wisdom that comes from Your throne.

Lord, in the swirl of decisions and the weight of responsibility, let Your voice rise above every other. Speak into the silence when he is unsure. Interrupt the noise when he is overwhelmed. Let Your counsel cut through confusion and bring clarity to every matter of governance and judgment. Where pride would blind or fear would paralyze, may Your Spirit correct, comfort, and counsel him in righteousness.

Establish within him a deep reverence for Your Word. Let it not be a token, but a treasure. Cause him to delight in Your law day and night, that he might be like a tree planted by streams of water, bearing fruit in due season, not withering under pressure. Surround him with wise, God-fearing advisors who walk in truth and not in deceit, and remove every voice of falsehood and manipulation from his midst.

Father, we plead that his leadership would be marked not by the applause of men, but by alignment with heaven. May Your counsel be the unseen hand directing his steps, shaping his policies, and guarding his legacy. Let his conscience be tender toward You. And when he stumbles, restore him with mercy. When he succeeds, keep him humble. When he wearies, strengthen him with Your presence.

Lord, we ask not for a perfect man, but for a leader governed by Your perfect will. Let his life and leadership reflect that he is guided by something higher than office—by You, the God of all wisdom and glory.

In Jesus' name, Amen.

SECTION 2:
AGAINST DISLOYAL INSIDERS

In every leadership journey, one of the greatest challenges comes not only from external opposition but from those within—those who betray trust, sow discord, or work quietly against the good of the nation. Section 2, *Against Disloyal Insiders*, confronts this hidden battle that can weaken even the strongest leader.

Our prayers in this section focus on the spiritual protection and strength needed for the President to stand firm amidst treachery and division. We ask God to expose secret schemes, guard hearts, and replace disloyalty with steadfast faithfulness. As we intercede, we stand in the gap, believing that God's righteous hand will uphold His chosen leader and thwart every attempt to undermine his mission.

This is a call to vigilance and spiritual warfare—because the enemy often attacks from within. Yet, by God's grace, loyalty will prevail, truth will shine, and the purposes of God for this nation will be accomplished. Let us pray with boldness and faith, standing shoulder to shoulder for our President in this critical hour.

Day 18: Expose the Traitor

> Yes, my own familiar friend, in whom I trusted, who ate bread with me, has lifted up his heel against me. But you, Yahweh, have mercy on me, and raise me up, that I may repay them. By this I know that you delight in me, because my enemy doesn't triumph over me. As for me, you uphold me in my integrity, and set me in your presence forever.
> —Psalms 41:9-12 WEB

Righteous Father,

You who see all things and know every hidden motive—You who search the hearts of men—we come before You with reverence and urgency. Your Word says, *"Even my close friend, someone I trusted, one who shared my bread, has turned against me"* (Psalm 41:9). Lord, we bring before You the burden of betrayal that lingers in high places, the unseen threats from those once trusted within the circle of leadership.

We stand in the gap for the President of this nation, crying out for Your divine protection from treacherous insiders. Where loyalty has been poisoned by personal gain, ambition, or manipulation, we ask You to uncover it. Bring to light every hidden scheme, every whisper in secret rooms, and every deceitful alliance. Let no betrayal escape Your justice.

Preserve the soul of the leader You have placed in office. Raise him up, as Your Word declares: *"But You, Lord, have mercy on me; raise me up, that I may repay them"* (Psalm 41:10). May his response be led by righteousness and not retaliation. May Your mercy shield him and Your truth guide him.

We declare by faith: *"In my integrity You uphold me and set me in Your presence forever"* (Psalm 41:12). Uphold him, O God, by Your hand.

Surround him with those whose hearts are pure, whose counsel is wise, and whose loyalty is rooted in Your truth.

Let righteousness be established, and treachery be exposed. Let Your justice prevail.

In Jesus' name, Amen.

Day 19: Bind Their Tongues

> Hide me from the conspiracy of the wicked, from the noisy crowd of the ones doing evil; who sharpen their tongue like a sword, and aim their arrows, deadly words, to shoot innocent men from ambushes. They shoot at him suddenly and fearlessly. They encourage themselves in evil plans. They talk about laying snares secretly. They say, "Who will see them?" They plot injustice, saying, "We have made a perfect plan!" Surely man's mind and heart are cunning. But God will shoot at them. They will be suddenly struck down with an arrow. Their own tongues shall ruin them. All who see them will shake their heads.
> —Psalms 64:2-8 WEB

Deliver our President, O God, from the secret counsel of the wicked, from insidious plots of disloyal insiders who shoot their words like arrows in the dark. They sharpen their tongues like swords, aiming bitter speech like ambushes without cause. You see every hidden whisper, every scheming thought masked in loyalty but bred in treachery. We plead with You—expose every lying tongue and double heart that seeks to undermine righteous leadership.

Rise up, O Righteous Judge, and shoot Your arrows of truth. Let their own words ensnare them. Let their prideful plans unravel by Your hand. You alone search the hearts and test the motives of men; uncover every act done in shadow to corrupt the integrity of this nation's leadership. Let not betrayal prosper. Let not the schemes of false counsel take root.

Silence the voices that sow confusion and division around the President. Surround him with those who fear You, who walk in truth, who are loyal not just to office but to righteousness. Let Your justice cause the nations to tremble, and let all men see that Your hand defends the one You have placed in authority.

In Jesus' name, Amen.

Day 20: SHIELD THE TRUSTWORTHY

> Oh how great is your goodness, which you have laid up for those who fear you, which you have worked for those who take refuge in you, before the sons of men! In the shelter of your presence you will hide them from the plotting of man. You will keep them secretly in a dwelling away from the strife of tongues.
> —Psalms 31:19-20 WEB

O Lord, our faithful and covenant-keeping God, how abundant is Your goodness, which You have stored up for those who fear You and worked for those who take refuge in You, in the sight of the children of mankind. You are our refuge and our stronghold in times of political shaking and betrayal. You see the inner workings of leadership, the hearts of men, and the hidden motives no human eye can discern.

Today we stand in the gap on behalf of the trustworthy—those loyal servants You have positioned around the President for righteousness' sake. These are men and women who have not bent the knee to corruption, who fear You more than man, and who speak truth when flattery abounds. Shield them, Lord. Hide them in the secret place of Your presence from the plots of men. Conceal them in Your shelter from the strife of tongues, from sabotage and slander, from political ambush and the venom of deceitful insiders.

Let no weapon formed against them prosper. Let their integrity preserve them. Strengthen their hands to carry out justice and support what is right without compromise. Surround them with favor as with a shield. Be their defense, their vindication, their silent witness.

May their loyalty be a lifeline to the nation's stability, a quiet channel through which Your purposes flow. As they honor the assignment, honor them with divine protection, wisdom, and lasting influence. Guard their families, their hearts, and their peace.

In Jesus' name, Amen.

Day 21: Purge the Wicked Council

For the Chief Musician. To the tune of "Do Not Destroy." A poem by David, when Saul sent, and they watched the house to kill him. Deliver me from my enemies, my God. Set me on high from those who rise up against me. Deliver me from the workers of iniquity. Save me from the bloodthirsty men. For, behold, they lie in wait for my soul. The mighty gather themselves together against me, not for my disobedience, nor for my sin, Yahweh. I have done no wrong, yet they are ready to attack me. Rise up, behold, and help me! You, Yahweh God of Armies, the God of Israel, rouse yourself to punish the nations. Show no mercy to the wicked traitors. Selah. They return at evening, howling like dogs, and prowl around the city. Behold, they spew with their mouth. Swords are in their lips, "For", they say, "who hears us?" But you, Yahweh, laugh at them. You scoff at all the nations. Oh, my Strength, I watch for you, for God is my high tower. My God will go before me with his loving kindness. God will let me look at my enemies in triumph. Don't kill them, or my people may forget. Scatter them by your power, and bring them down, Lord our shield.
—Psalms 59:1-11 WEB

O God our Strength and Deliverer,

We cry out to You on behalf of the one You have set in leadership over this nation. Deliver him, Lord, from those who rise up against him—

those who plot treachery in secret, waiting like prowling dogs in the night. See how they lie in wait, speaking twisted things with arrogant lips, yet You, O God, see all things and are not silent.

Arise, Mighty One, and confront the wickedness that seeks to surround and sabotage the President. Expose every scheming voice, every manipulative hand, and every rebellious heart that pretends to serve while plotting betrayal. Cut off their influence. Let not the traitor sit at his table or the liar whisper in his ear.

You are the God who sees through pretenses—break through every false counsel and hidden agenda with Your light and Your truth.

O Lord of Hosts, defend him not because of his perfection, but because of Your unfailing love and covenant purposes for this land. Scatter those who mock righteousness. Remove those who slander in secret. Silence every voice that seeks to devour with words like swords.

Be his fortress when he is weary, and his shield when arrows fly by day.

Let his eyes be turned toward You, not shaken by the howling of foes or the mutterings of dissent. Let his heart find its strength in Your justice and his joy in Your steadfast mercy. Rule over his enemies, Lord—do not slay them at once, but strip them of power, one by one, so that the people may see and know that You, O God, reign in this nation.

Establish loyal voices around him—wise, upright, faithful men and women who fear Your name. Raise up a council shaped by truth, not ambition—by Your Spirit, not by self-gain. Let every decision be hemmed in by divine discernment, and every step guarded by angels on assignment.

You are our Refuge in times of trouble. Let every snare be turned against the snare-setter, and every plan that is not from You be brought to nothing. Surround the President with Your song of deliverance, and let Your name be honored through righteous leadership in our land.

In Jesus' name, Amen.

Day 22: DESTROYED BY THEIR PERVERSENESS

> The integrity of the upright shall guide them, but the perverseness of the treacherous shall destroy them.
> —Proverbs 11:3 WEB

Righteous Judge and Sovereign Lord,

We come before You, bearing the burden of leadership in this nation, crying out for the one You have placed in authority. Your Word declares in Proverbs 11:3, *"The integrity of the upright shall guide them: but the perverseness of transgressors shall destroy them."* Father, we plead for Your hand to move mightily in the halls of power, especially in the President's inner circle.

We cry out against the perverseness that plots in secret—the deceitful advisors, the hidden betrayers, and the ones who feign loyalty while sowing corruption. Lord, expose every perverse counsel and silence every lying tongue that seeks to manipulate leadership for wicked gain. Let no unrighteous influence stand unchecked. Tear down strongholds of deception and division that would destroy the vision You've entrusted to our nation's leadership.

But Father, also grant discernment to the President. Let integrity be the guiding light, and truth the standard. Surround him with men and women of righteousness, who fear You and not man. Uproot disloyalty and replace it with faithfulness. Let every decision be aligned with Your justice and carried on the foundation of moral courage.

We stand in the gap, Lord, not in our strength but in full dependence on You. Have mercy. Deliver. Cleanse the inner circle of corruption and raise up a shield of loyalty around our leader. Fulfill Your purpose in this hour.

In Jesus' name, Amen.

Day 23: GUARD AGAINST DECEPTION

> For such men are false apostles, deceitful workers, masquerading as Christ's apostles. And no wonder, for even Satan masquerades as an angel of light.
> —2 Corinthians 11:13-14 WEB

Righteous Father, You who see all things in the light of Your truth,

We come before You in holy reverence, standing in the gap for the one You have appointed to lead this nation. We lift up our voice in intercession, crying out for divine protection against those who appear as ministers of righteousness but are, in truth, deceivers—false apostles and cunning workers, as Your Word declares in 2 Corinthians 11:13-14. For Satan himself transforms into an angel of light, and so do his servants disguise themselves to deceive and to destroy.

Lord, shine the piercing light of Your truth into every place of hidden corruption. Expose every lie, every counterfeit loyalty, every smooth word that masks betrayal. Shield the heart of our President from being ensnared by those who seek access only to manipulate, subvert, or divide. Strengthen him in discernment, that he may know those who walk in truth and those who wear the mask of deception.

Let no charm or flattering speech disarm his vigilance. Let no counterfeit counsel sway his convictions. Root out the Judas spirit within the ranks and surround him instead with voices of truth, wisdom, and integrity—men and women filled with the Spirit of God and committed to righteousness.

We plead the blood of Jesus as a covering over his mind, decisions, and inner circle. Let Your truth reign, and let Your Spirit lead him in every step. Guard the gate of his trust, and let only the faithful enter in. In Jesus' name, Amen.

Day 24: WISDOM TO DETECT LIES

> A truthful witness will not lie, but a false witness pours out lies.
> —Proverbs 14:5 WEB

Righteous Father, You are the God of truth, and no falsehood can stand in Your presence. You declared in Your Word, *"A faithful witness does not lie, but a false witness breathes out lies"* (Proverbs 14:5). We come before You, standing in the gap for our President and the leadership You have appointed, asking for divine wisdom to discern truth from deception. In a time where loyalty is tested and betrayal hides in shadows, we plead for light to expose every false witness and hidden agenda.

Lord, surround our President with faithful witnesses—men and women of integrity who love truth more than power and righteousness more than reward. Uproot every disloyal insider, every whisperer and deceiver whose counsel is not from You. Let every false testimony be uncovered, and let every hidden lie be brought into the open by the power of Your Spirit.

Grant the President a discerning heart like Solomon's—to detect manipulation, to perceive motives, and to judge righteously. May Your truth be his shield and buckler. Let no scheme of darkness prosper against Your plans for this nation. Guard him from the snares of flatterers and the subtle traps of betrayal. Raise up loyal voices who speak with clarity, courage, and conviction.

We trust You, Sovereign Lord, to defend the righteous and to silence the deceiver. Let Your truth prevail in the highest courts and secret councils.

Let justice roll down like waters, and righteousness like a mighty stream.

In Jesus' name, Amen.

Day 25: Root Out Hidden Schemes

> For I have heard the defaming of many, "Terror on every side! Denounce, and we will denounce him!" say all my familiar friends, those who watch for my fall. "Perhaps he will be persuaded, and we will prevail against him, and we will take our revenge on him." But Yahweh is with me as an awesome mighty one. Therefore my persecutors will stumble, and they won't prevail. They will be utterly disappointed, because they have not dealt wisely, even with an everlasting dishonor which will never be forgotten. But, Yahweh of Armies, who tests the righteous, who sees the heart and the mind, let me see your vengeance on them; for to you I have revealed my cause.
> —Jeremiah 20:10-12 WEB

Righteous Judge and Defender of the upright,

We come before You with trembling hearts, standing in the gap for the one You have appointed to lead this nation. You see all things—what is whispered in shadows, what is plotted behind closed doors, what is veiled in loyalty but reeks of betrayal. Just as Jeremiah cried out, surrounded by those who sought his downfall, so too does our President face voices of treachery, men and women who wait for his stumble, who whisper, *"Perhaps he will be deceived, then we will prevail against him."*

But You, O LORD, are with him as a mighty, awesome One. Let those who plot against him stumble and not prevail. Let their schemes be exposed and turned to confusion. May their dishonor be everlasting, never forgotten—not for vengeance, but that truth would be upheld, and that righteousness would rule from the highest seat in the land.

Search the heart and mind, O LORD of hosts, You who test the righteous. Root out every hidden agenda, every false counselor, every voice that masks manipulation behind friendship. Raise up loyal hearts, wise advisors, and men and women of truth who will strengthen his hands for justice and mercy.

We declare that the President shall not be ensnared by traps laid in secret. Shield him with discernment. Surround him with integrity. Let Your truth march before him like a flame, and let all deception be driven out by the light of Your presence.

In Jesus' name, Amen.

Day 26: DELIVER FROM BETRAYAL

> For it was not an enemy who insulted me, then I could have endured it. Neither was it he who hated me who raised himself up against me, then I would have hidden myself from him. But it was you, a man like me, my companion, and my familiar friend. We took sweet fellowship together. We walked in God's house with company. Let death come suddenly on them. Let them go down alive into Sheol. For wickedness is among them, in their dwelling. As for me, I will call on God. Yahweh will save me.
> —Psalms 55:12-16 WEB

O Lord God, our Shield and our Deliverer,

We come before You with heavy hearts, standing in the gap for our President and the leaders You have appointed in this nation. Your Word says, *"For it was not an enemy who reproached me; then I could bear it... But it was you, a man my equal, my companion and my acquaintance. We took sweet counsel together, and walked to the house of God in the throng"* (Psalm 55:12-14). Father, the sting of betrayal is sharp, and it often comes from those closest—those trusted with access, counsel, and loyalty.

We ask You now, Sovereign God, expose every hidden agenda, every voice cloaked in friendship but filled with deceit. Uproot every plant not planted by You. Remove from the President's inner circle those who plot evil, who sow confusion, and who work against Your divine assignment. Let truth and integrity be the standard, and surround him with those who fear Your Name and walk in righteousness.

Lord, as David cried, *"As for me, I will call upon God, and the Lord shall save me"* (Psalm 55:16), so we cry out to You for deliverance. Deliver our President from Judas-like betrayal. Shield him from whispering lips and divisive spirits. Be his lifeline in moments of secret attack.

Raise up intercessors to stand watch. Let angels encamp around him. And may Your purpose for this nation prevail through loyalty, wisdom, and divine protection.

In Jesus' name, Amen.

Day 27: Don't Let Them Rejoice

They also who seek after my life lay snares. Those who seek my hurt speak mischievous things, and meditate deceits all day long. But I, as a deaf man, don't hear. I am as a mute man who doesn't open his mouth. Yes, I am as a man who doesn't hear, in whose mouth are no reproofs. For in you, Yahweh, do I hope. You will answer, Lord my God. For I said, "Don't let them gloat over me, or exalt themselves over me when my foot slips." For I am ready to fall. My pain is continually before me. For I will declare my iniquity. I will be sorry for my sin. But my enemies are vigorous and many. Those who hate me without reason are numerous. They who also render evil for good are adversaries to me, because I follow what is good. Don't forsake me, Yahweh. My God, don't be far from me. Hurry to help me, Lord, my salvation.
—Psalms 38:12-22 WEB

Lord God Almighty,

You who know every heart and every hidden scheme, I come before You today standing in the gap for our President. You see the battles waging not only outside but within—the whispers, the disloyalty, the insiders who would seek to undermine and overthrow the trust placed in him. Father, the psalmist cries out, "They also that seek after my life lay snares; and they that seek my hurt speak mischievous things." Protect him from those who rejoice at his downfall and plot in secret to harm the work You have called him to do.

Strengthen his heart when fear and weariness threaten to overwhelm; lift him when pain presses heavy upon his soul. Let not the words of enemies cause him to stumble or lose courage. Instead, be his refuge and fortress. Sustain him with Your righteousness and truth, that his loyalty to You and this nation may stand firm and unwavering.

Turn the hearts of those who seek to betray into vessels of repentance and peace, or bring Your justice to bear swiftly and rightly. Let no shadow of disloyalty triumph, and let Your divine purpose for this presidency be fulfilled unhindered. May Your Spirit guide his every decision, guard his integrity, and surround him with faithful counsel.

In the midst of trials, grant him courage to persevere, knowing that You are near and that victory belongs to You alone. Do not let those who delight in his pain rejoice, but cause their plans to fail, and bring Your glory forth through his leadership.

In Jesus' name, Amen.

Day 28: SILENCE THE WHISPERERS

> A perverse man stirs up strife. A whisperer separates close friends.
> —Proverbs 16:28 WEB

Lord God,

You are the righteous Judge who sees every hidden word and every secret whisper. I come before You now, standing in the gap for our President, asking You to silence the whisperers who stir strife and division within his circle. You have warned us that "a perverse person stirs up conflict, and a gossip separates close friends." Protect him from those whose words seek to fracture loyalty and undermine his leadership from the inside.

Surround him with Your peace that surpasses all understanding, and let Your truth be his shield against deception and slander. Shut down every tongue that speaks falsely, every heart that plots in darkness, and every scheme designed to cause confusion or betrayal. Strengthen his spirit to rise above the noise, to discern wisely, and to lead with integrity rooted in Your wisdom.

Let unity and faithfulness prevail among those who serve him, and bring healing where discord has taken root. Turn the hearts of the disloyal toward repentance, or expose their plans so they cannot succeed. May Your glory be revealed through a leadership fortified by Your strength and protected by Your hand.

We trust in Your sovereign power to guard our President against every attack from within, and we pray that Your kingdom purposes for this nation will stand firm, unshaken by whispers and strife.

In Jesus' name, Amen.

Day 29: PROTECT THE FAITHFUL

> Many men claim to be men of unfailing love, but who can find a faithful man?
> —Proverbs 20:6 WEB

Lord God,

You are the One who knows every heart and sees beyond what eyes can discern. We come before You now, standing in the gap for the faithful insiders who surround our President—those rare and precious souls whose loyalty, integrity, and steadfastness keep the wheels of leadership turning in Your perfect order. You declare in Your Word that many claim loyalty, but who can find the faithful? We ask You, Father, to protect these faithful ones with Your divine shield.

Strengthen their resolve in the face of temptation and deceit. Guard their hearts against weariness and discouragement when the pressure mounts and the enemy's schemes grow more cunning. Let their loyalty not be in vain; let their counsel be wise and their words seasoned with Your truth. Surround them with Your peace and courage, that they may stand strong as pillars of righteousness amid swirling storms of disloyalty.

Preserve them from harm, whether seen or unseen. Give them discernment to navigate treacherous waters and the grace to remain humble and dependent on You alone. May their faithfulness be a lifeline to the President, a source of encouragement, and a beacon of hope in this pivotal hour.

Father, let Your kingdom purposes be fulfilled through their unwavering loyalty. May they flourish and be honored in Your sight, as they uphold justice, truth, and godly leadership. We place them into Your hands, trusting in Your perfect care.

In Jesus' name, Amen.

Day 30: GUARD THE NATION'S SECRETS

> One who brings gossip betrays a confidence, but one who is of a trustworthy spirit is one who keeps a secret.
> —Proverbs 11:13 WEB

Righteous Father, we come before You as watchmen on the walls, interceding for our nation and its leaders. Your Word declares in Proverbs 11:13, *"One who brings gossip betrays a confidence, but one who is of a trustworthy spirit is one who keeps a secret."* Lord, we plead with You to raise up faithful men and women around our President—those who walk in integrity and truth, who fear Your name more than the opinions of man, and who protect that which is sacred and strategic to this nation.

We cry out on behalf of the leadership You have placed over us. Surround the President with counselors who are loyal not only to their assignment but to You, the One who establishes all authority. Expose every talebearer, every deceiver, every hidden agent of betrayal who seeks to manipulate, leak, or destroy from within. Shut the mouths of those who whisper in dark corners and trade the nation's confidence for personal gain.

Let there be no breach in the wall of security and no compromise in the counsel he receives. Strengthen the inner circle with discernment and spiritual vigilance. May every person given access to the corridors of power be tested by fire and proven faithful. Let the spirit of truth prevail in the inner chambers of leadership, and let no unfaithful voice rise above the sound of wisdom and righteousness.

Lord, we repent on behalf of a nation that has too often tolerated the compromising of secrets and sacred trusts. Cleanse the places of influence from corruption, and let the fear of the Lord be restored in every level of government. Silence the voice of betrayal, and raise up faithful intercessors to stand in the gap, declaring Your Word, Your ways, and Your will over this land.

We trust in Your justice and in Your ability to root out every hidden thing. You are the God who sees, the God who reveals, and the God who protects. Let Your hand be upon this nation and its President to uphold righteousness, guard the purposes You have ordained, and keep the gates from being opened to the enemy.

In Jesus' name, Amen.

Day 31: Exile the Faithless

> God is a righteous judge, yes, a God who has indignation every day. If a man doesn't repent, he will sharpen his sword; he has bent and strung his bow. He has also prepared for himself the instruments of death. He makes ready his flaming arrows. Behold, he travails with iniquity. Yes, he has conceived mischief, and brought out falsehood. He has dug a hole, and has fallen into the pit which he made. The trouble he causes shall return to his own head. His violence shall come down on the crown of his own head.
> —Psalms 7:11-16 WEB

Righteous and Holy God,

You are a just Judge, burning with indignation every day against the wicked. You see all things hidden and exposed—every betrayal, every deception, every heart turned against Your appointed order. You are not silent, and You do not slumber. You rise with judgment in Your hand, and You test the hearts and minds of men.

Lord, we come before You in the spirit of Psalm 7, standing in the gap for our President and the leadership You have allowed to stand. We cry out for Your divine intervention against disloyal insiders—those who dig pits of treachery, who bend their bows with lies, and set traps with flattering tongues. Let them fall into the very holes they have dug. Let their mischief return upon their own heads. Do not let their violent schemes prosper.

Father, uproot the unfaithful from within the house. Expose those who wear the garments of allegiance but harbor rebellion. Purge the counsel around our leaders, and raise up voices who walk in truth and integrity. Let righteousness be their shield and Your justice their rear guard.

You are a shield to those who walk uprightly. Surround the President with loyal, wise, and God-fearing men and women. Silence the voice of the accuser and bring down every false confidant. Cut off access to those who have sold their hearts for personal gain. You see their end—how they conceive trouble and birth falsehood. Deliver our nation from their plans.

Lord, be the lifeline of our leadership. Let the blood of the innocent no longer cry out from the ground, and may treachery not reign in the inner courts. Build a hedge of holy fire around our leaders and cast out every Judas spirit. We plead for mercy, but we cry for Your justice. We ask for healing, but we trust in Your sword to make the way straight.

Raise up Daniels and Josephs. Cast down Ahithophels and Jezebels. Strengthen the hands of the faithful, and bring swift discipline upon those who have mocked Your name by pretending allegiance. Let Your justice roll down like waters and Your righteousness like a mighty stream in this land.

In Jesus' name, Amen.

Day 32: EXPOSE HIDDEN MOTIVES

> The heart is deceitful above all things and it is exceedingly corrupt. Who can know it? "I, Yahweh, search the mind. I try the heart, even to give every man according to his ways, according to the fruit of his doings."
> —Jeremiah 17:9-10 WEB

O Righteous Father, Searcher of all hearts,

Your Word declares in Jeremiah 17:9-10 that the heart is deceitful above all things and desperately wicked—who can know it? But You, O Lord, You search the heart and examine the mind to reward each person according to their conduct, according to what their deeds deserve.

We come before You as intercessors, standing in the gap for the leadership of this nation, and especially for the President whom You have allowed to hold office in this hour. Lord, we cry out for Your divine discernment and unshakable truth to reign in the corridors of power. Expose every hidden motive and every secret agenda that stands against Your plans and purposes for this land. Tear the veil from hearts that harbor betrayal, selfish ambition, and deception. Let no whisper in the dark go unnoticed before You, O God who sees in secret.

Father, raise up a wall of protection around the President from those who sit at the same table but plot in their hearts to undermine, to manipulate, and to destroy. Reveal the hearts of those who smile in public but scheme in private. You are the God who tests the mind and tries the reins—do what only You can do. Uproot every false allegiance and lay bare every counterfeit loyalty.

Let righteousness and truth surround the President like a shield. Purify the inner circle. Let only those whose hearts are aligned with Your will remain. Bring swift conviction where repentance is possible, and removal where there is rebellion. Deliver our President from the hands of disloyal insiders and fill every seat of counsel with men and women who fear You above all else.

We do not rely on the wisdom of men, but on You—the all-seeing, all-knowing Judge of the earth. You weigh the thoughts and intents of the heart. Let Your justice thunder through the halls of power, and let Your mercy be extended to those who turn back to You.

Let no deception endure in Your light. Let no darkness withstand the fire of Your holiness. May the plans of the wicked unravel before they are birthed, and may the nation be spared the fruit of hidden iniquity. We plead for divine exposure—for the sake of righteousness, for the preservation of godly leadership, and for the lifeline of a nation under God.

In Jesus' name, Amen.

Day 33: UPHOLD THOSE OF GOOD CONSCIENCE

> Pray for us, for we are persuaded that we have a good conscience, desiring to live honorably in all things.
> —Hebrews 13:18 WEB

Righteous Father,

We come before You with reverence and trembling, lifting our voices on behalf of the leaders who stand closest to the President of this nation. Your Word in Hebrews 13:18 says, "Pray for us: for we trust we have a good conscience, in all things willing to live honestly." So Lord, we stand in agreement with this holy plea. We intercede now for those surrounding the President—advisors, cabinet members, counselors, and all who hold positions of influence near him.

Uphold those whose hearts are guided by integrity. Strengthen the ones who walk in good conscience and desire to serve with honesty and righteousness. Let Your Spirit bear witness in them, confirming truth and exposing every hidden motive. Shield them from corruption, from weariness, from compromise. Let their loyalty be first to You, Almighty God, and from that loyalty let wise and just counsel flow.

We ask You to expose disloyalty, deceit, and double-mindedness. Let no saboteur remain hidden in the shadows. Cut off the influence of those who speak one thing before men but another behind closed doors. Raise up bold truth-tellers who fear You more than man. Place around the President men and women of godly conscience—those who will stand even when it costs, who will speak life, wisdom, and conviction born of Your Spirit.

Father, we plead for discernment in leadership. Let the President see through flattery and manipulation. Surround him with the Daniels and Esthers of our time—those who will fast, pray, and speak what is right in the courts of power. Let righteous voices rise above the noise. Let loyalty to You be their lifeline, and truth be their language.

Strengthen the weary ones who have not bowed to corruption. Encourage them, O God. Cover them in Your peace. Let them know that You see their sacrifices and will reward their faithfulness. Pour out wisdom and clarity upon them, that they may not only stand, but prevail.

We declare Your Word, that in all things they will live honestly, governed by a conscience awakened by Your truth. Uphold them, Lord. Defend them. Surround them with Your angels, and let no weapon formed against them prosper.

In Jesus' name, Amen.

Day 34: GOD, OUR REFUGE FROM TREACHERY

> *For the Chief Musician. For a stringed instrument. By David.*
> Hear my cry, God. Listen to my prayer. From the end of the earth, I will call to you, when my heart is overwhelmed. Lead me to the rock that is higher than I. For you have been a refuge for me, a strong tower from the enemy. I will dwell in your tent forever. I will take refuge in the shelter of your wings. Selah. For you, God, have heard my vows. You have given me the heritage of those who fear your name. You will prolong the king's life; his years shall be for generations. He shall be enthroned in God's presence forever. Appoint your loving kindness and truth, that they may preserve him.
> —Psalms 61:1-7 WEB

Hear my cry, O God; attend unto my prayer. From the ends of the earth I call to You with a heart overwhelmed by the weight of betrayal and inner strife. You alone see the hidden counsels of the disloyal, those who wear the garments of unity but harbor division in their hearts. Lord, lead us to the Rock that is higher than we are—stable, unshakable, and pure.

You have been a shelter for this nation and a strong tower from the enemy. We come to You on behalf of our President, surrounded not only by opposition without, but by treachery within. Raise up righteous voices and expose the subtle undermining of authority. Let loyalty be found in the inner circle; let truth be the bond that holds counsel together.

Let the President abide in Your tabernacle forever; cover him under the shadow of Your wings. Preserve him from the schemes of those who disguise ambition as advice and manipulation as loyalty. May Your mercy and truth continually preserve him. Strengthen his heart, Father, and sustain his leadership with wisdom that comes from above.

You have heard our vows, O God. We will not cease to cry out for justice, for integrity, for divine covering. Appoint angels to stand watch where men cannot be trusted. Let Your presence be the fortress no enemy can breach. Lift up the weary arms of Your servant and surround him with those whose hearts are set on Your purpose, not personal gain.

So will we sing praise unto Your name forever, fulfilling our vows daily as watchmen on the wall. Let this nation see Your hand at work through leaders who fear You and walk in truth.

In Jesus' name, Amen.

SECTION 3:
AGAINST ASSASSINATION ATTEMPTS

There are few assignments more sacred—or more contested—than national leadership. Throughout history, those chosen to lead have been marked by both divine purpose and intense opposition. The higher the calling, the greater the warfare.

Assassination, whether by physical violence, political sabotage, or spiritual attack, is a demonic attempt to cut off God's plans before they can be fulfilled. As intercessors, we are not called to fear these threats, but to confront them boldly through prayer.

This section is a direct engagement with the forces of darkness that seek to destroy life, destabilize leadership, and derail divine destiny. These are not passive prayers—they are declarations of war against every scheme of death, exposure of hidden plots, and release of divine protection. You will pray with the authority of heaven for angelic intervention, supernatural preservation, and God's mighty hand to be a shield around the President day and night.

Now is the time to stand in the breach, to cry out like watchmen on the wall, and to believe that no weapon formed will prosper. The enemy may plot, but God is greater. His plans will prevail—and your prayers are part of that victory. Let's lift our voices in faith and stand guard through intercession.

Day 35: HELP AGAINST THE KILLERS

> The Philistines had war again with Israel; and David went down, and his servants with him, and fought against the Philistines. David grew faint; and Ishbibenob, who was of the sons of the giant, the weight of whose spear was three hundred shekels of brass in weight, he being armed with a new sword, thought he would kill David. But Abishai the son of Zeruiah helped him, and struck the Philistine, and killed him. Then the men of David swore to him, saying, "Don't go out with us to battle any more, so that you don't quench the lamp of Israel."
> —2 Samuel 21:15-17 WEB

O Sovereign Lord, Mighty Defender of the helpless and Shield of the righteous,

We come before You today as those who stand in the gap for our leaders—especially for the one You have placed as the head of this nation. You are the same God who preserved David in his weariness when the enemy sought to strike him down. Just as Abishai rose to defend the king and slew the giant Ishbi-Benob, so we now rise in the Spirit to war in prayer for the protection of our President.

Lord, You see the unseen threats. You know the hidden counsels of the wicked. You see those who, like the descendants of the giants, are plotting destruction and death. But You are our strong tower. You are the God who delivers from the snare of the fowler and from the deadly pestilence. We cry out to You—shield our President from every plot of assassination, from physical harm, from every scheme born in darkness and aimed with hatred.

Father, when the leaders You have chosen grow weary, when the burden becomes heavy and the strength of man is not enough, raise up intercessors like Abishai—faithful, loyal, alert, and full of courage. Let us not be passive in prayer, but fierce in the Spirit, standing with authority and discernment to intercept every attack of the enemy. Let our prayers strike down every spiritual Ishbi-Benob that seeks to extinguish the lamp of leadership You have lit.

We declare by faith that no weapon formed against him shall prosper. We plead the blood of Jesus over every place he walks, every room he enters, every journey he takes. Send Your angels to encamp round about him. Thwart every plot. Expose every scheme. Paralyze every assignment of death. We say, "Not on our watch," O God! For as long as You give us breath, we will stand and fight in prayer.

Preserve the lifeline of this nation's leadership. Do not allow the lamp to be quenched. Protect him not only from physical danger but from the spirit of fear and despair. Let courage, wisdom, and supernatural alertness be his portion. Let him know that there is a praying people lifting him up daily before Your throne.

We stand, Lord, not in our own strength, but in the name of Jesus—the One who triumphed over every principality and power. Stretch out Your hand, O God. Let Heaven's army move now to deliver and defend.

In Jesus' name, Amen.

Day 36: SHADOW OF DEATH, FEAR NOT

> Even though I walk through the valley of the shadow of death,
> I will fear no evil, for you are with me. Your rod and your staff,
> they comfort me.
> —Psalms 23:4 WEB

Most Holy and Sovereign Lord,

We come before You today as watchmen on the wall, intercessors appointed to cry out for the soul of this nation and for the life and destiny of its appointed leader. Father, You are our Shepherd, and because of that, we shall not want. Even now, as we walk through the valley of the shadow of death, we will fear no evil—for You are with us. Your rod and Your staff, they comfort us.

Lord, we lift up the President of the United States before You, the one whom You have allowed to be placed in a seat of authority for such a time as this. We cry out against every dark scheme, every demonic assignment, and every plotted assassination attempt—whether physical, political, or spiritual. Let every weapon formed against him be broken and made of no effect. Hide him in the secret place of the Most High. Cover him under the shadow of Your wings. Let Your angels encamp round about him and deliver him.

Though the shadow of death may loom and threats may arise in hidden places, You, O God, are greater than the darkness. You are the Light that no shadow can overcome. May Your presence go before him, stand behind him, and surround him on every side. Let no fear grip his heart, for perfect love casts out fear. Strengthen him with might in his inner man; give him wisdom and discernment to navigate treacherous paths. Speak peace to his soul and courage to his spirit.

God of justice, expose every trap. Reveal every traitor. Uproot every wicked plan before it takes root. Let Your rod correct and guide, and let Your staff pull him back to safety when the path grows narrow. May he feel Your nearness in the midnight hours, when burdened with decisions too great for man. You are with him, O Lord. Let him not only know it, but walk in the strength of that truth.

We plead the blood of Jesus over his life, his family, his mind, and his assignment. We declare that no weapon formed against him shall prosper and every tongue that rises against him in judgment, You shall condemn. For this is the heritage of the servants of the Lord.

We trust You, Shepherd of our souls. Lead our nation and its leader through the shadowed valley into the light of Your righteousness and Your purposes.

In Jesus' name, Amen.

Day 37: VAULTED IN GOD'S ARMS

> "There is no one like God, Jeshurun, who rides on the heavens for your help, in his excellency on the skies. The eternal God is your dwelling place. Underneath are the everlasting arms. He thrust out the enemy from before you, and said, 'Destroy!'
> —Deuteronomy 33:26-27 WEB

Father,

We come before You with trembling hearts and steadfast faith, standing in the gap for the leader You have placed over this nation. We cry out for divine protection, for supernatural shielding, for a vaulting of Your presence around the President. Let no weapon formed against him prosper. Let no plot of darkness advance beyond Your reach. Cover him under the shadow of Your wings. Let him dwell in safety in the refuge of the Most High.

Lord, You are the God who defends. You are not distant. You are near, leaning in with power and compassion. Vault him, O God, in Your arms—arms that do not falter, arms that do not grow weary, arms that have carried Israel and now carry us. Place Your fiery glory between him and every assassin's aim, between him and every snare of death, between him and every lying tongue.

We call on You, Mighty Deliverer—displace every force of wickedness. Confuse the conspiracies. Scatter the camps of darkness. Let every hidden thing be exposed and uprooted. Let no evil pass through the fortress of Your will.

Preserve him, O God, not only in body, but in soul and calling. Let him trust not in chariots or horses, but in the name of the Lord his God. Let him know that You, Eternal One, are his refuge. Let him abide in You, and may the prayers of the saints rise continually as incense before Your throne on his behalf.

We do not trust in the arm of the flesh. We trust in You—the Ancient of Days, the Defender of destiny, the Keeper of covenant. Our hope is not in earthly means, but in Your divine intervention. Stretch forth Your hand, O Lord, and surround him with loyal watchers, angelic and earthly, assigned and awakened.

We proclaim: the President is vaulted in God's arms. He will not fall. He will not die, but live to declare the works of the Lord in the land of the living.

In Jesus' name, Amen.

Day 38: WATCHTOWER OVER OUR HEAD

> *For the Chief Musician. For a stringed instrument. By David.*
> Hear my cry, God. Listen to my prayer. From the end of the earth, I will call to you, when my heart is overwhelmed. Lead me to the rock that is higher than I. For you have been a refuge for me, a strong tower from the enemy.
> —Psalms 61:1-3 WEB

Lord of Hosts, Defender of the righteous,

We come boldly before Your throne, standing in the gap for the leader You have set over this nation. You are the Sovereign Watchman who never slumbers nor sleeps. We ask You now to rise in Your might and stretch forth Your arm to cover the President with Your divine protection. Let no weapon formed against him prosper. Let every scheme of darkness be scattered by the light of Your presence.

O Lord, we plead the blood of Jesus over every pathway he walks, every space he enters, and every plan he sets forth. Station Your angels round about him as flames of fire—stand them on every side as guards of Your holiness and power. Confuse the communications of those who plot harm; disrupt the devices of those who seek his life. Break the bow of the wicked and cut the cords of the oppressor. Let the counsel of Ahithophel be turned into foolishness, and may the secret plans of the enemy fall into their own traps.

We cry to You, the Rock higher than we are, asking You to be a shelter over the head of our leader. Be his refuge and fortress, his God in whom he trusts. Let Your truth be his shield and buckler. Cover him with Your wings, hide him in the secret place of the Most High, and preserve his soul from evil. Let no sudden terror overtake him. Let no evil befall him. Let every plot of assassination dissolve under the weight of Your justice.

Raise up watchmen on every wall—spiritual and natural—who will not hold their peace day or night. Awaken a company of intercessors who will cry out for life, mercy, and divine intervention. Cause loyalty to be established among his advisors and bodyguards. May every person in his sphere be filled with discernment and the fear of the Lord.

Lord, we appeal to You not only for preservation, but for purpose. Guard his life so that Your plans may be fulfilled through him. Establish him as a vessel of justice, truth, and righteousness in the land. Let him not be moved, for You are his strong tower.

We declare with confidence: You, O God, are the shield about him—his glory, and the lifter of his head.

In Jesus' name, Amen.

Day 39: NO HURT SHALL COME

> "Behold, I have created the blacksmith who fans the coals into flame, and forges a weapon for his work; and I have created the destroyer to destroy. No weapon that is formed against you will prevail; and you will condemn every tongue that rises against you in judgment. This is the heritage of Yahweh's servants, and their righteousness is of me," says Yahweh.
> —Isaiah 54:16-17 WEB

Most High God, Sovereign over all the earth, we come before You with trembling hearts and holy boldness, standing in the gap for our President, the one You have placed in authority over this nation. You alone form the smith who blows the coals in the fire, and You create the weapon that is fashioned for its purpose—yet You, O Lord, also declare that no weapon formed against Your servants shall prosper. We cling to Your Word, trusting in Your absolute authority over every plot, every scheme, and every evil device fashioned in darkness against our President.

Lord, we appeal to Your divine justice and mercy. You see what is hidden, You expose what is concealed, and You thwart the plans of the wicked before they can take form. We ask that every conspiracy, every whisper in secret rooms, every shadowy plan of violence or betrayal be uncovered and destroyed by the light of Your presence. Let the power of Your truth be a shield around him. Let Your angels be stationed as watchmen upon his path, bearing swords of fire to guard his going out and his coming in.

Father, let no hurt, no harm, no wound come near him. We silence every lying tongue that rises in judgment, every curse, every death sentence spoken in malice or rebellion—we refute them now by the inheritance of Your servants. You have promised vindication from You, and we declare it over the President of this nation. Guard his mind, body, and spirit; keep him from the snare of the fowler and the deadly pestilence.

We plead the blood of Jesus over him as a banner of triumph and a covering of divine safety. May every day of his purpose be fulfilled under Your hand. May no man, no force, no principality interrupt the plans You have ordained through him. Let him walk in loyalty to You, and may his heart remain tethered to the lifeline of Your Spirit.

Raise up Your intercessors across this land to pray without ceasing, to build a wall of fire around the leader You have appointed, and to stand firm until Your will is done. For You, O God, are faithful. You are the Defender. You are the Avenger of Your anointed.

In Jesus' name, Amen.

Day 40: FRUSTRATE WICKED DEVICES

> He frustrates the plans of the crafty, So that their hands can't perform their enterprise.
> —Job 5:12 WEB

Righteous and Sovereign Lord,

You are the One who frustrates the devices of the crafty, so that their hands cannot carry out their plans. You see what is done in secret and bring it to light. Nothing is hidden from Your eyes. You alone are God, enthroned above all principalities and powers, ruling in justice and truth.

Today, I stand in the gap for our President and for this nation under Your covering. I cry out to You as an intercessor, lifting a holy plea before the courts of heaven: Frustrate the plans of the wicked. Disarm the schemes of the violent. Confuse the counsels of those who plot evil in secret, and scatter their gatherings in confusion. Let their words fall to the ground. Let their weapons never prosper. Render powerless every device of assassination, sabotage, and destruction that has been forged in the shadows against the leader You have appointed.

Father, arise and contend with those who contend with righteousness. Surround our President with divine protection—let angels encamp around him day and night. Let every hidden trap be exposed before it is set. Let every plan of darkness be turned into foolishness by Your mighty hand. Cancel the enemy's assignments and uproot every seed of treachery and betrayal from within and without.

You are our Shield and Defender, the God who saves by His outstretched arm. So we call on You, Jehovah Sabaoth—the Lord of

Hosts—to wage war in the spirit against all who would rise in opposition to Your purpose for this nation. Let the plans of the enemy be turned back upon themselves. Let peace prevail where violence was intended. Let life flow where death was plotted.

We put our trust in You, O God, who preserves the lives of Your servants. Let Your will be done on earth as it is in heaven. Let Your name be glorified in the preservation of leadership, in the triumph of justice, and in the establishment of truth in this land.

In Jesus' name, Amen.

Day 41: Eyes Guarding Day and Night

> He will not allow your foot to be moved. He who keeps you will not slumber. Behold, he who keeps Israel will neither slumber nor sleep. Yahweh is your keeper. Yahweh is your shade on your right hand. The sun will not harm you by day, nor the moon by night. Yahweh will keep you from all evil. He will keep your soul. Yahweh will keep your going out and your coming in, from this time forward, and forever more.
> —Psalms 121:3-8 WEB

O Sovereign Keeper of Israel, who never slumbers nor sleeps, we come before You with earnest hearts, standing in the gap for the President of this nation. According to Your Word, You are the One who will not allow our foot to be moved. You are our shield, our shade at our right hand. And so, we cry out for Your divine protection over the life of the President—body, soul, and spirit.

Lord, You are the Keeper who watches by day and by night. Let Your eyes that never close be ever fixed upon him. Frustrate every hidden plot, dismantle every scheme of darkness, and expose every agenda of violence before it can be set into motion. Let every assassin's weapon be disarmed by Your unseen hand. Let the arrows that fly by day and the terror that lurks by night be rendered powerless under the authority of Your name.

You have said that You will preserve our going out and our coming in from this time forth, and even forevermore. We claim this promise over the President's every journey, every appearance, every meeting, every moment. Assign Your angels, O God, to encamp round about him and deliver him from all harm. Place a hedge of fire and favor around him and those who walk in righteousness with him.

We declare that the sun shall not strike him by day, nor the moon by night. Not by natural threats, not by spiritual warfare—nothing shall prevail against him when You are his Keeper. Fortify his mind, strengthen his resolve, and guard his heart with supernatural peace. Let him walk under the canopy of Your sovereign care, shielded by the intercession of the saints and the unyielding love of the God who watches over him.

Let every life-giving purpose You have ordained through his leadership come to pass. And let no weapon formed against him prosper, because You, Lord, are his defense and mighty deliverer.

In Jesus' name, Amen.

Day 42: GOD IS OUR REFUGE

For the Chief Musician. By the sons of Korah. According to Alamoth. God is our refuge and strength, a very present help in trouble. Therefore we won't be afraid, though the earth changes, though the mountains are shaken into the heart of the seas; though its waters roar and are troubled, though the mountains tremble with their swelling. Selah.
—Psalms 46:1-3 WEB

Most High God, our refuge and strength, an ever-present help in trouble—today we stand in the gap for our President, lifting him before Your throne of mercy. You alone are our safe place, our impenetrable fortress in times of threat. We cry out on behalf of our nation's leader, asking that You would surround him with Your divine protection. Let no weapon formed against him prosper. Let every scheme of the enemy be exposed and dismantled before it can take form.

Though the nations rage and the earth gives way—though chaos and threats may rise like the roaring sea—we will not fear, for You, O Lord, are with us. You are the God of Jacob, our stronghold. Hide our President under the shadow of Your wings. Fortify every place he walks, every vehicle he enters, every room he occupies. Dispatch Your angels, Lord—mighty, warring angels—to guard him in all his ways.

Silence every voice of violence. Halt every hand of destruction. Confound every plot and confuse every conspirator. Where evil lurks in darkness, bring Your light and truth to expose it. Let every plan against his life be turned back on the heads of those who devised it, not by vengeance, but by justice and Your righteous hand.

You are our refuge—our mighty God who cannot be shaken. Let the hearts of Your intercessors remain steadfast, knowing You are in the midst of our pleas. We call upon You not only for protection, but for peace—the peace that surpasses understanding to rest upon our leader, even in the face of threats. Be his confidence, be his shield, be his rear guard.

In the day of trouble, You are near. In the hour of crisis, You remain enthroned. Therefore, we will not fear. We will trust in Your name, the name above every other name.

In Jesus' name, Amen.

Day 43: ENCOMPASSED BY HIS WINGS

> "...May Yahweh repay your work, and a full reward be given to you from Yahweh, the God of Israel, under whose wings you have come to take refuge." He will cover you with his feathers. Under his wings you will take refuge. His faithfulness is your shield and rampart.
> — Ruth 2:12; Psalms 91:4 WEB

Most High God, our Refuge and our Fortress, we come before You with reverence and boldness, standing in the gap for the leader You have set in place for this nation. Your Word declares in Ruth 2:12, *"The Lord recompense thy work, and a full reward be given thee of the Lord God of Israel, under whose wings thou art come to trust."* And again, in Psalm 91:4, *"He shall cover thee with His feathers, and under His wings shalt thou trust: His truth shall be thy shield and buckler."*

Father, we lay hold of these promises now as we lift up our President before You. Surround him, O Lord, with Your mighty wings—encompass him with divine protection. Hide him in the shelter of Your presence. Let no weapon formed against him prosper. Let every scheme of darkness be uncovered and brought to nothing. Frustrate the devices of the crafty, so that their hands cannot perform their enterprise. Let angelic forces stand guard day and night, intercepting every plot of violence or premature death.

We plead the precious blood of Jesus over him—body, soul, and spirit. Shield him from every sniper's aim, from every hidden trap, from every spirit of death and destruction that would seek to cut off his destiny and abort Your plans for this nation. Be a wall of fire around him, and the glory in his midst. Let every hour, every public appearance, every journey be covered by the wing of Your providence.

Lord, You are not a man that You should lie. You are faithful to Your covenant. You have promised that under Your wings we find trust and refuge, and that Your truth is our shield and our buckler. So we declare Your Word over our President—he shall not die, but live, and declare the works of the Lord. Let this be a testimony to the nations that the God of Israel still watches over those who put their trust in Him.

We will not fear the terror by night, nor the arrow that flies by day, for You are with us. You are with him. You are faithful. You are mighty to save.

In Jesus' name, Amen.

Day 44: DIVINE ESCORT ON THE WAY

> For he will put his angels in charge of you, to guard you in all your ways. They will bear you up in their hands, so that you won't dash your foot against a stone.
> —Psalms 91:11-12 WEB

Most High God, Almighty and Sovereign King,

We come before You with holy reverence, acknowledging that You are our refuge and fortress, our God in whom we trust. With hearts bowed and spirits stirred, we lift up the President of this nation—Your appointed leader in this hour—and we take our place in the gap on their behalf.

Lord, You have said in Your Word that *"He will command His angels concerning you to guard you in all your ways; they will lift you up in their hands, so that you will not strike your foot against a stone."* We cling to this promise with faith unshaken. Command Your angels now, Father. Release Your heavenly host to surround the President like a shield. Let them encamp around every motorcade, every entrance, every path they take. Station them on rooftops, in shadows, in rooms where threats may plot. Let no harm befall Your servant.

We stand in the authority of Christ Jesus, and we renounce every scheme, every ambush, every plan of assassination conceived in darkness. We declare that the blood of Jesus speaks a better word—one of protection, deliverance, and destiny fulfilled. Let every arrow aimed in secret break before it is launched. Let every snare be exposed and destroyed. May those who plot violence be brought to repentance or removed from their positions of harm.

Father, lift the President high above every danger, unseen and seen. Let no weapon formed against them prosper. Let the President walk under divine escort—not only of trained guards but of angelic forces sent directly from Your throne. In meetings, on the road, in the quiet hours—guard their life. Shield their mind. Preserve their purpose.

We ask not for man's security, but for heaven's defense. Wrap Your servant in glory, clothe them in divine protection, and let their days be lengthened that Your will for this nation may go forth without delay.

We stand in faith, unshaken and unyielding, and we will not relent.

In Jesus' name, Amen.

Day 45: PROLONG THE KING'S LIFE

> You will prolong the king's life; his years shall be for generations.
> —Psalms 61:6 WEB

Righteous Father, Sovereign over all nations, we lift our voices to You in earnest intercession. Your Word declares in Psalm 61:6, *"You will prolong the king's life, his years as many generations."* We cling to this promise, crying out to You for divine preservation over the one appointed to lead this nation. We stand in the gap, O God, asking that You stretch forth Your mighty hand and shield the President from every plot of darkness, from every scheme of violence, from every attempt of assassination and destruction.

Let no weapon formed against him prosper. Let every snare laid in secret be exposed by Your light and rendered powerless by Your authority. Place around him the fire of Your protection, legions of angels standing guard day and night. Be his fortress, his refuge, his defender. Thwart every plan of the enemy and let confusion confound those who rise against him.

We ask for health in his body, clarity in his mind, and strength in his soul. Renew him daily, Lord. Cause his years to be many, not for vain ambition, but that he may fulfill all You have ordained for him in righteousness and truth. As long as his assignment remains, let his life be upheld by Your mercy, his decisions guided by Your wisdom, and his heart aligned with Your will.

Establish him in loyalty to You and loyalty to justice. Let his leadership be marked by integrity, compassion, and courage. May he dwell under the shadow of the Almighty, secure in the shelter of Your wings.

Hear this cry, O God of our salvation. For the sake of a people, for the sake of a nation, for the sake of Your name—preserve the life of the king.

In Jesus' name, Amen.

Day 46: HIDDEN FROM THE SNARE

> For in the day of trouble, he will keep me secretly in his pavilion. In the secret place of his tabernacle, he will hide me. He will lift me up on a rock.
> —Psalms 27:5 WEB

Most High God, our Refuge and Strength, we come before You with reverence, humility, and urgency, lifting up our President, the one You have appointed to lead this nation. Lord, You are the Sovereign Keeper of life, and Your Word declares in Psalm 27:5 that in the time of trouble, You shall hide us in Your pavilion; in the secret place of Your tabernacle, You shall hide us, and You shall set us high upon a rock.

We call upon that promise now, Father. Hide the President in Your divine pavilion. Let no evil reach him, no scheme of darkness prevail, no weapon of assassination find its mark. Shield him, O God, with Your holy covering. Let every plot be exposed, every snare be broken, every ambush be overturned by the power of Your hand. Surround him with angels on every side—heaven's guard standing watch day and night.

We cry out for divine interception of every plan conceived in secret. Let those who seek harm be scattered in confusion, and let their plans fall to the ground, void and powerless. Let the counsel of the wicked be as nothing, and let Your counsel alone stand in this nation.

Preserve his life, Lord. Extend his days in health and strength. Let him walk in the vitality that comes from Your presence, and may he live to see the goodness of the Lord in the land of the living. Strengthen his heart, uphold him with Your righteous right hand, and let him not fear though war may rise against him.

In the secret place of the Most High, keep him hidden. In the tabernacle of Your mercy, let him abide. Place him high upon the rock—Christ Jesus—beyond the reach of destruction. Protect his body, mind, and soul. Let no illness, no infirmity, and no hidden threat take root. Let the blood of Jesus speak a better word over him.

We pray with fervor, with faith, and with the full confidence of Your Word, knowing that You are a God who delivers, who preserves, and who watches over the lives of those You have called.

In Jesus' name, Amen.

Day 47: GUARDED BY ANGELS

> Yahweh's angel encamps around those who fear him, and delivers them.
> —Psalms 34:7 WEB

O Lord of Hosts, Mighty Deliverer and Shield of Your people, we come before You with trembling hearts and fervent cries, standing in the gap for the one You have appointed to lead this nation. Your Word declares in Psalm 34:7, *"The angel of the Lord encamps around those who fear Him, and He delivers them."* We hold fast to this truth and cry out for Your divine protection over the President.

Father, station Your angels—mighty and swift—to encamp round about him day and night. Let their swords of fire ward off every plan of destruction, every whisper of assassination, every hidden scheme of darkness. Expose the traps before they are set. Confuse the tongues that plot evil in secret. Let no weapon formed against him prosper, and let every tongue that rises in judgment be condemned, for this is the heritage of the servants of the Lord.

Lord, let a hedge of divine fire surround him wherever he goes—whether by land, air, or sea. May his steps be ordered by You, and may his security be anchored in Your supernatural hand. Let the discernment of Your Spirit fall upon those assigned to guard him, that no detail be missed and no breach go undetected.

We plead the blood of Jesus over his mind, body, and spirit. Strengthen him with long life and preserve his health with Your sustaining power. Renew his strength like the eagle's; keep him sharp in wisdom, unwavering in truth, and faithful in his calling. Let him not grow weary in doing good, and may Your favor be a shield around him as with a mighty buckler.

God of Abraham, Isaac, and Jacob, rise up and defend Your servant. Let not the purposes for this nation be thwarted by violence or chaos. Let righteousness and peace be his portion, and may Your justice prevail. In every room he enters, may Your presence go before him. In every decision he makes, may Your counsel be his guide.

We stand in faith, unshaken, declaring that he is guarded by angels, delivered by Your hand, and covered in covenant grace. Do this, O Lord, not for our sake, but for the honor of Your great name, that the nations may know You are God.

In Jesus' name, Amen.

Day 48: EXPOSED SCHEMES FOILED

> Finally, brothers, pray for us, that the word of the Lord may spread rapidly and be glorified, even as also with you; and that we may be delivered from unreasonable and evil men; for not all have faith. But the Lord is faithful, who will establish you, and guard you from the evil one.
> —2 Thessalonians 3:1-3 WEB

Righteous and Sovereign Lord,

We come before You as intercessors, standing in the gap for the one You have placed in leadership over this nation. Father, just as Paul urged the saints to pray that the word of the Lord may run swiftly and be glorified, we ask that Your purposes for our President would be fulfilled without delay or hindrance. Let every plan You have ordained come to pass, unhindered by evil men or destructive schemes.

Lord, You are faithful. You will establish him and guard him from the evil one. In the authority of Jesus Christ, we declare that every hidden plot, every whispered conspiracy, every demonic assignment sent to assassinate or harm the President is now exposed, dismantled, and rendered powerless. Shine Your light into the darkness and foil every plan formed in secret. Let confusion fall upon the camp of the wicked. Let their networks break and their traps backfire.

Lord, let every wicked scheme plotted in darkness against the President be exposed by the light of Your truth. Tear off the veil of secrecy from those who plot assassination and destruction. Let their conspiracies fall like brittle walls under the weight of Your justice. Frustrate the tokens of liars. Strip the confidence from the wicked. Cause confusion in their camps. Reveal, unravel, and reverse every assignment of death and chaos.

We declare, Lord, that no weapon formed against the President shall prosper, and every tongue that rises in judgment You shall condemn. You are his Keeper, his Shield, his Rock of defense. Let Your angelic hosts encamp round about him, guarding him in all his ways. Let those who seek his life fall into the traps they have set. Turn their counsels into foolishness, and scatter their alliances.

Strengthen the President's inner man with courage, discernment, and unwavering loyalty to Your voice. Establish his steps in righteousness and cover him with the full armor of God. Guard his going out and coming in. Raise up righteous advisors and remove every Judas from his circle. Let Your Word have free course through his leadership—that it may run swiftly and be glorified in this land.

Father, not all have faith, but we trust in Your faithfulness. You are able to establish and protect him from the evil one. You are the Deliverer, the Revealer, the Foiler of plots, and the Guardian of purpose.

In Jesus' name, Amen.

Day 49: No Unlawful Plot Prevails

> There is no wisdom nor understanding nor counsel against Yahweh. The horse is prepared for the day of battle; but victory is with Yahweh.
> —Proverbs 21:30-31 WEB

Almighty God, Sovereign Lord of Heaven and Earth, we come before You today, standing in the gap for the leader You have appointed over this nation. With hearts bowed in humility and faith, we declare Your Word: *"There is no wisdom, no insight, no plan that can succeed against the Lord. The horse is made ready for the day of battle, but victory rests with the Lord."* (Proverbs 21:30-31)

Father, we lift up the President to You. You alone establish kings and remove them. You alone ordain times and seasons. And so, in the authority of Your Word, we decree that no unlawful plot, no wicked scheme, no weapon formed in secret or in plain sight shall prosper against the one You have set in leadership. Where there are councils of darkness plotting violence, expose them, scatter them, and render their devices useless. Let confusion fall in their camp and their strategies fall to the ground like dust.

You are the God who sees all and knows all. You frustrate the plans of the crafty so that their hands achieve no success. Frustrate every plan of assassination, sabotage, or destruction. Cover the President with divine protection—let angels encamp around him. Be a wall of fire around him and the glory within. Let every assignment of death be overturned by the resurrection power of Jesus Christ.

We pray for long life and sustained health for the President. Let his body be strengthened daily. May he walk in vitality, wisdom, and divine clarity. Let no disease, no illness, no sudden attack prosper against his life. Be his strength in the day of adversity and his peace in the storm.

Though human strength may prepare, though security may stand watch, we acknowledge that true safety comes from You. You are our defense. You are our victory. So we entrust this leader into Your hands, declaring that Your purpose for his life and leadership will not be aborted, delayed, or destroyed. Raise up intercessors and watchmen to continually stand guard in the Spirit.

Let the plans of the Lord prevail, for Your counsel stands forever. We trust in You, and we place this nation's leadership under the shadow of Your wings.

In Jesus' name, Amen.

Day 50: SAFE IN HIS CARE

> David spoke to Yahweh the words of this song in the day that Yahweh delivered him out of the hand of all his enemies, and out of the hand of Saul, and he said: "Yahweh is my rock, my fortress, and my deliverer, even mine; God is my rock in whom I take refuge; my shield, and the horn of my salvation, my high tower, and my refuge. My savior, you save me from violence. I call on Yahweh, who is worthy to be praised; So shall I be saved from my enemies.
> —2 Samuel 22:1-4 WEB

Most High God, our Rock and our Deliverer, we come before You in deep humility and fierce faith, standing in the gap for the life and safety of our nation's President. Just as David declared in the day You delivered him from all his enemies, so we declare now with boldness and trust: You are our fortress, our stronghold, and our refuge. You are the shield that surrounds those who put their trust in You, the horn of salvation, and the high tower of protection.

Lord, we cry out to You—not as strangers, but as sons and daughters who know Your voice and trust Your covenant. We call upon You, worthy to be praised, and we declare: the President shall be saved from his enemies. Every hidden plot, every whisper in the dark, every snare set by the enemy to cut short his days—we cancel them now in the name of Jesus.

Father, stretch forth Your mighty hand and surround him with angels encamped round about him. Let the walls of Your salvation rise up around him like fire. Expose and dismantle every assignment of assassination, sabotage, or harm, whether by hand, by word, or by unseen forces. Confuse the counsel of the wicked and turn their weapons back upon themselves.

You, O Lord, are a shield for him, his glory and the lifter of his head. Even when he is unaware, You are aware. Even when he sleeps, You do not slumber. Place him under the shadow of Your wings. Let him be safe in Your care, hidden in the cleft of the Rock. May he dwell securely in the place of Your choosing, far from the reach of evil, guarded by Your name.

Let the song of deliverance rise over his life, and let the nation witness the power of a God who defends His appointed. May his safety be a sign to the people that You still reign, that You still answer prayer, and that You still raise up leaders for Your purposes.

We trust You, Sovereign Lord. We exalt You as our shield and strong deliverer.

In Jesus' name, Amen.

Epilogue

Fifty days. Fifty prayers. Fifty moments of standing in the gap for one of the most influential positions in the world. If you've journeyed through this book, then you've done more than just read—you've engaged in battle. You've stood between the living and the dead. You've lifted up the President, the leadership of this nation, and the destiny of a people before the throne of Almighty God.

Your prayers have not been in vain. Heaven hears. Angels move. Darkness trembles when a believer dares to pray in alignment with God's will. You may never know on this side of eternity the full impact of your intercession, but rest assured: lives have been spared, decisions have been influenced, and divine protection has been released because you chose to stand in the gap.

This assignment may be complete, but the call remains. Continue to pray. Continue to watch. Continue to believe. Our leaders need it. Our nation needs it. God honors it.

Stand strong. Stay faithful. And never stop praying.

What Happens Next?

1. **Keep Praying.**
   Revisit these prayers as needed. Use them during election cycles, national days of mourning or celebration, or when the news headlines grow heavy. Prayer is not seasonal—it is eternal.

2. **Go Deeper.**
   Let this spark fuel a lifestyle of watchfulness. Begin to pray for your local leaders, school boards, police, churches, and neighborhoods. God is not only concerned with nations—He's concerned with every person who lives in them.

3. **Mobilize Others.**
   Start a prayer group. Share what you've learned. Invite your church, youth ministry, or Bible study into this mission. Prayer is contagious—and right now, our nation needs an outbreak of it.

4. **Trust God's Timing.**
   Not every answer will come immediately, and not every shift will be visible. But the Word is clear: *"The prayer of a righteous person is powerful and effective"* (James 5:16). God is working—even in silence.

A Final Word of Hope

Remember, the battle for a nation is won first and foremost in the realm of prayer and spiritual surrender. Your prayers have not been in vain.

Keep this flame of intercession burning in your heart beyond these pages. Let it ignite a lifelong commitment to seek God's will for your nation, your community, and your own life. Trust that the God who commands the heavens and the earth is also guiding the steps of those who place their hope in Him.

May you continue to be a watchman on the walls, a voice for justice, and a bearer of peace. And may the nation whose God is the Lord be blessed now and forevermore.

In Jesus' name, Amen.

ENCOURAGE OTHERS WITH YOUR STORY

If this prayer guide has strengthened your faith, deepened your intercession, or helped you stand in the gap for our nation, would you consider leaving a short review on Amazon? Your feedback not only encourages others but also helps more believers discover this resource and join in praying for this nation. Every review—just a few sentences—makes a difference and helps spread the call to stand in the gap. Thank you for being part of this movement.

MORE FROM PRAYERSCRIPTS

STANDING IN THE GAP FOR COVENANT AWAKENING:

30 DAYS OF PRAYER FOR NATIONAL REPENTANCE, RIGHTEOUS LEADERSHIP & GOD'S SOVEREIGN RULE

What if your prayers could help turn the tide of a nation?

America stands at a spiritual crossroads. Division deepens, truth is under siege, and righteousness is being redefined. But God is still searching for those who will stand in the gap—intercessors who will cry out for mercy, justice, and national awakening.

Standing in the Gap for Covenant Awakening is a 30-day prayer guide for believers who sense the urgency of the hour and long to see their nation return to God.

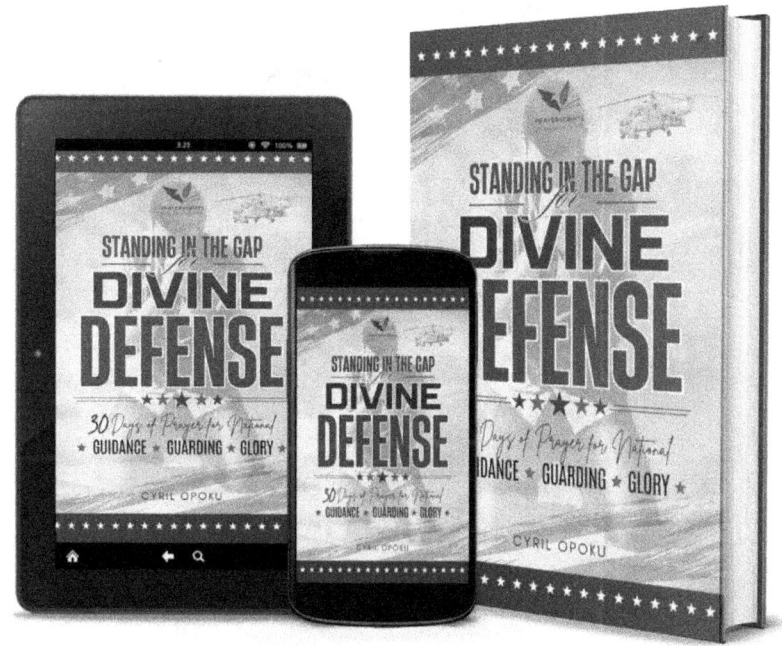

STANDING IN THE GAP FOR DIVINE DEFENSE:

30 DAYS OF PRAYER FOR NATIONAL GUIDANCE, GUARDING & GLORY

When the foundations of a nation feel as if they're shaking, prayer is the strongest fortress you can build.

Standing in the Gap for Divine Defense: 30 Days of Prayer for National Guidance, Guarding & Glory is your call to action—a 30-day journey of powerful, Scripture-rooted intercession that invites everyday believers to become watchmen on the walls for their nation. Drawing on timeless truths from God's Word, this devotional equips you to stand in the gap for your nation and **Seek Heaven's Wisdom, Secure Divine Protection,** and **Ignite Spiritual Awakening.** If you sense the urgency of the hour and long to see your country guided and guarded by the hand of God, open these pages. Stand in the gap. Watch Him move.

STANDING IN THE GAP FOR NATIONAL HEALING:

40 DAYS OF PRAYER FOR RECONCILIATION, RIGHTEOUSNESS, AND RESTORATION

What if your prayers could help heal a nation? What if God is waiting for someone—like you—to stand in the gap?

Standing in the Gap for National Healing: 40 Days of Prayer for Reconciliation, Righteousness, and Restoration is a bold, Spirit-filled call to action for believers who refuse to sit on the sidelines while their nation drifts further from God. In a time marked by division, confusion, and moral decline, this book equips you to pray with power, precision, and unshakable hope. Inside, you'll find 40 days of Scripture-based intercession divided into three strategic sections: **Peace, Unity & Reconciliation, Morality, Truth & Righteous Leadership**, and **National Restoration & Reformation**. It's time to stop watching history unfold—and start shaping it in prayer.

Scriptures & Prayers for Deliverance from Trouble:
40 Days of Prayer for When Life Feels Overwhelming

Are you walking through a season where life feels heavy, hope feels distant, and your prayers feel weak?

Scriptures & Prayers for Deliverance from Trouble is a 40-day journey of honest prayers and powerful Scriptures to help you find peace, strength, and healing when life is overwhelming. Each day offers a personal, Scripture-based prayer written in the language of real faith and raw trust. This devotional isn't about perfect words—it's about real connection with God when you need Him most.

SCRIPTURES & PRAYERS FOR DELIVERANCE FROM EVIL:
50 DAYS OF PRAYER TO OVERCOME DARKNESS AND FIND GOD'S PROTECTION

When darkness presses in, how do you pray?

When fear grips your heart or unseen battles rage around you, you need more than generic words—you need Scripture, truth, and the steady hand of God to lead you through.

Scriptures & Prayers for Deliverance from Evil: 50 Days of Prayer to Overcome Darkness and Find God's Protection is a powerful devotional journey designed to help you pray boldly and biblically through seasons of spiritual warfare, oppression, fear, or uncertainty.

SCRIPTURES & PRAYERS FOR ENGAGING THE ENEMY:

70 DAYS OF PRAYER TO REBUKE THE ENEMY AND RELEASE GOD'S POWER

You weren't called to run from the battle—

you were anointed to win it.

Scriptures & Prayers for Engaging the Enemy: 70 Days of Prayer to Rebuke the Enemy and Release God's Power is a bold devotional for believers who are ready to rise, resist, and reclaim what the enemy has tried to steal. If you're tired of feeling spiritually outnumbered, this book will equip you to fight back—with Scripture in your mouth and power in your prayers. Over 70 days, you'll be guided through five strategic phases of spiritual warfare: (1) Rebuking the Enemy, (2) Releasing Terror Upon the Enemy (3) Praying for the Fall of the Enemy (4) Treading Upon the Enemy (5) When Heaven Strikes.

The war is real. But so is your victory.

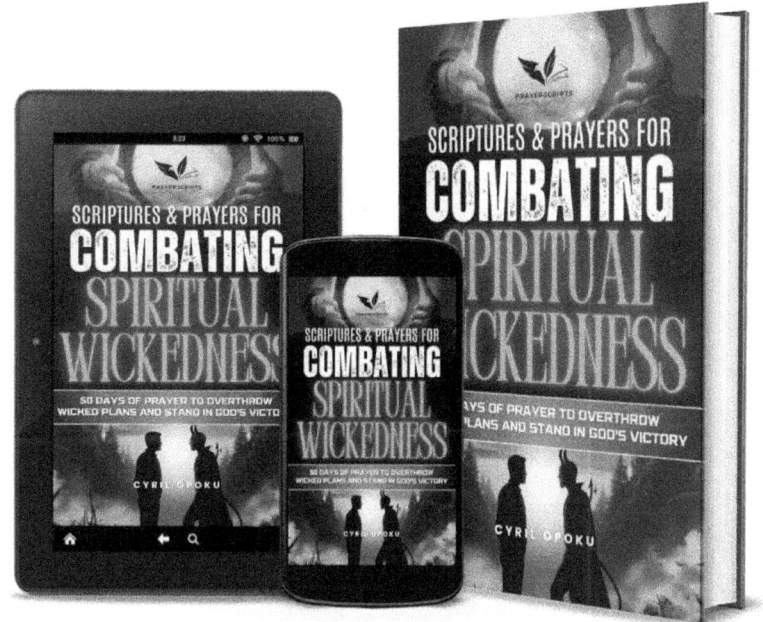

SCRIPTURES & PRAYERS FOR COMBATING SPIRITUAL WICKEDNESS:
50 DAYS OF PRAYER TO OVERTHROW WICKED PLANS AND STAND IN GOD'S VICTORY

Are you facing opposition that feels deeper than the natural? Do you sense hidden resistance working against your progress, peace, or purpose? You're not imagining it—and you're not powerless.

Rooted in the authority of Scripture and fueled by bold, targeted prayers, *Scriptures & Prayers for Combating Spiritual Wickedness* equips you to confront darkness head-on. Each day features a focused Bible passage and a heartfelt, Scripture-based prayer designed to nullify ungodly counsel, disrupt demonic schemes, and establish God's victory in every area of your life.

www.ingramcontent.com/pod-product-compliance
Lightning Source LLC
Chambersburg PA
CBHW060815050426
42449CB00008B/1665